THEOLOGY PRIMER

Resources for the Theological Student

JOHN JEFFERSON DAVIS

Baker Book House
Grand Rapids, Michigan 49506

Copyright 1981 by
John Jefferson Davis

ISBN: 0-8010-2912-0

First printing, August 1981
Second printing, June 1983

Library of Congress
Catalog Card Number: 81-67093

Chapter 4, "Truth: Philosophical and Theological Issues,"
was prepared for *The Tyndale Encyclopedia of Christian Knowledge*.
Copyright © by Tyndale House Publishers, Inc., Wheaton, Ill.
Used by permission. All rights reserved.

Printed in the United States of America

Contents

Preface

The beginning student in theology may feel overwhelmed by the massive amount of theological literature that has been produced during two thousand years of Christian history. The *Theology Primer* is intended to help the student to find his or her way around the theological landscape, and to facilitate the task of locating the theological resources needed for the work of ministry. The "Guidelines for Theological Research, Reflection, and Expression" are designed to assist the student in developing skills for applying biblical and theological principles to practical situations in ministry. A "Brief Glossary of Theological Terms" gives capsule definitions of a number of technical terms which may be unfamiliar to the new student. A "Brief Guide to Modern Theologians" gives concise sketches of the lives and positions of a number of theologians whose names are likely to be encountered by the theological student. "Truth: Philosophical and Theological Issues," may be helpful particularly to those with little previous background in theology and philosophy. The "Bibliography" includes significant books that are

5

likely to be useful in a first-unit course in systematic theology.

Any manual such as this is bound to reflect the limitations inherent in the constraints of space and the writer's selective choices. Nonetheless, it is hoped that this small volume will prove to be a handy reference tool both for the student and for those now engaged in the work of ministry.

John Jefferson Davis

1

Guidelines for Theological Research, Reflection, and Expression

Christian theology was born in the context of the existential needs of ministry in the church. New converts needed to be catechized in preparation for full membership, heretical teachings threatening the faith and unity of the church had to be combated, and all members needed instruction in the sound doctrine essential to growth in Christian maturity. In the context of seminary education, which all too often gives the impression of being unrelated to the actualities of church ministry, it is good for teacher and student alike to recall this existential focus of Christian theology.

As the title indicates, this discussion concerns theological research, reflection, and expression. While some in the ministry may do little in the way of formal research, theological reflection and expression are inescapable. One cannot preach a sermon or teach a Sunday-school lesson or counsel a parishioner without at least implicitly reflecting in a coherent way on the content of Scripture and its application to the contemporary needs of the church. The purpose of formal training in theology is to sharpen one's skill in performing these functions. Given the fact that theological reflection will occur in any case, it is the presumption here that it is desirable to do this in as informed and coherent a fashion as our abilities, training, and circumstances will permit.

Theological expression can be in oral or written form: a sermon, a lesson, a pastoral conversation, a term paper would be common examples. In the following discussion, the primary concern is for written expression, especially research papers, but many of the considerations would be of general applicability. In keeping with our concern to relate theological reflection and ministry, we begin with a situation that could easily arise in today's church.

Situation

You are the pastor of a small evangelical church in a Midwestern town. One of the elders of your church, who is also a member of the local school committee, comes to your office to seek counsel on a decision which he must make within the week. The town has become agitated by widespread rumors that Mr. _____, a popular social-studies teacher in the high school, is a practicing homosexual. In a private interview with the school committee Mr. _____ stated that he was indeed a practicing homosexual, but that, in his view, his private life had no bearing on his performance as a teacher, and that his lifestyle was not in conflict with the teaching contract requiring "personal integrity" and "conduct in keeping with community standards." He has indicated that the American Civil Liberties Union is prepared to file suit against the school committee for personal harassment if a move is made for dismissal. Would you advise your elder to vote for dismissal? Would you advise some other course of action? In a pluralistic society, how do biblical values relate to policy decisions which affect non-Christians?

Analysis

Definitional Phase (Planning)

The process of theological reflection appropriately begins with a definition of the problem. Can the problem be stated clearly in the form of a question, or several concise questions? Putting the issue in question form helps us to focus in our own minds various aspects of what may be a rather complex reality. What exactly is it that I am trying to decide? In this case we might ask, "How do my convictions as a Christian on the subject of homosexuality relate to a policy decision affecting an unbeliever?" Since it is frequently helpful to attempt to generalize the issue at hand, we might ask, "To what extent are moral principles based on Scripture suitable as legislative norms in a pluralistic society?" By generalizing the question this way, we can see from the outset that our research and reflection could bear fruit in other areas of contemporary concern beyond the immediate horizon of our problem, for example, abortion, divorce, or in vitro fertilization. It is in fact the case that true research—in contrast to merely "cranking out a paper"—opens our minds to new horizons and intellectual vistas not anticipated at the beginning of the process of reflection. All true learning is an encounter with the unknown, a venturing into uncharted waters, and is inherently risky—but also potentially very rewarding.

Now that we have focused the issue in question form, our next step in the definitional phase naturally moves to a consideration of key *terms*, *concepts*, and *distinctions*. It has been said that to define well is to think well. It has also been said that the making of distinctions is the key to success in theology. Both statements have a great deal to recommend them. From the very first moments of our postnatal existence, when we can scarcely distinguish our bodies from the outside world, until the moment of our death, the making of distinctions is vital to our effective functioning in the world. Hot and cold, smooth and sharp, male and female, food and poison—upon such distinctions our lives are predicated. It should come as no surprise, then, that becoming familiar with key terms, concepts, and distinctions plays a significant role in a first theology course. The "Brief Glossary of Theological Terms" has been developed with this need in mind.

In the case at hand, the terms *homosexuality* and *homosexual* are obviously central. Do I have a precise understanding of their meaning? Should I use the terms *homosexual* and *gay* interchangeably, or prefer one to the other? What about the distinction between homosexuality as a *practice* and homosexuality as a *tendency*? Is this distinction valid? Relevant? Other concepts such as *law, morality,* and *religion* will need attention. Can legal policy be separated from morality and/or religion? What about traditional distinctions among various types of law in the Old Testament, that is, *cultic, moral,* and *civil*? Further distinctions need to be considered in the matter of *sin* versus *crime*. What is the relation between the two? To what extent do they overlap? Then finally (at least at this juncture), the concepts of *conscience, general revelation,* and *common grace* call for analysis. How accountable is the unbeliever to the moral law? How much does he or she know prior to conversion?

At this point the beginning student may feel inclined to throw up hands in despair, saying, "How can I be expected to know what terms and distinctions are crucial in an area in which I haven't done much previous work?" This is a fair question, and it occurs to any researcher. We often proceed with only a vague idea of the solutions we are seeking, but with the conviction that we will recognize what we are looking for when we encounter it. In the meantime, we can only plunge into the subject matter of the problem, gradually acclimating ourselves to a new environment, gradually increasing our skill in finding our way around the new terrain. In spite of the outline suggested in this chapter, true research and discovery most often proceed not in a straight line, but in very uneven fits and starts. (For those of you who might be inclined to probe further the dynamics and psychology of the process of discovery—"heuristics"—I would recommend *Personal Knowledge: Towards a Post-Critical Philosophy*, by Michael Polanyi.)

Analytical Phase ("Input")

At this point in the investigation we are prepared to ask the question, "What types of information do I need, and where can I locate that information?" The answers to these questions have, at least implicitly, already been generated by the reflections on key terms, concepts, and distinctions in the first phase. In a Christian context we naturally turn to biblical passages dealing with homosexuality, civil law, general revelation, and conscience. Here we can make use of Bible dictionaries, encyclopedias, concordances, and commentaries. In many cases a Bible dictionary provides a convenient entry into a subject area, not only giving a general overview and survey of pertinent texts, but usually helpful bibliographic clues as well. This represents the exegetical dimension of the research. Various systematic theologies and theological monographs can help us see particular issues such as homosexuality in the wider context of biblical revelation, for example, the doctrine of man, law and grace, and the nature of sin.

For both the *exegetical* and *theological* dimensions of the investigation, periodical indices such as *Religion Index*

One: Periodicals (formerly *Index to Religious Periodical Literature*) and *New Testament Abstracts* are invaluable for locating journal articles dealing with a particular term or biblical text. A well-written journal article is one of the most helpful tools available for obtaining in a reasonably short period of time a sense of the previous scholarship in an area and the important lines of interpretation within it. For purposes of general orientation, a journal article can often be more helpful than a book. Journal articles also tend to represent the "state of the art" in scholarly research, in that specialized discoveries find their way into the journals before being incorporated into books, at least in most cases.

In assembling information it is important to consider the *historical* dimension. How have past generations understood issues similar to the one at hand? What analogies from history might shed light on our particular problem? What is the history of the church's opinions on the subject? If these opinions have changed or developed, what factors influenced the changes? Various theological encyclopedias listed in the bibliography in this book can be helpful at this point. A work like P. A. Sorokin's *Dynamics of Culture* contains much information on various patterns of law, religion, and morality in different historical periods. The *Encyclopedia of Philosophy* can be an entry into the area of natural law and its development over the centuries. Especially in a theologically conservative context, the student may be inclined to attempt to move directly from the biblical text to a contemporary solution, without considering or appreciating the intellectual labors of those in the past. Sometimes this attempt to overleap the past merely ends up in activities that "reinvent the wheel." Historical consciousness can be a real timesaver, and is a habit of mind that needs to be cultivated. If our first question is, "What does the Scripture teach on this subject," perhaps our second should be,

"What is the history of discussion on this issue?" There will be very few cases indeed where we can not profit from the labors of those who have preceded us.

Finally, as an essential component of this phase, the contemporary and empirical data pertinent to the case need consideration. What are the exact factual and circumstantial dimensions of the problem at hand? Are our assumptions about Mr. _____ in our case based on hearsay and rumor, or on reliable firsthand testimony? What are the particulars of the teaching contract and the laws of the community and state? Are there medical, psychological, and sociological studies on the subject of homosexuality that might inform our theological understanding and our pastoral practice? A journal article like Paul Cameron's "Case Against Homosexuality" (Human Life Review 4:3 [1978]: 17-49), is helpful at this point. While the controlling presuppositions of our human understanding and practice of ministry are drawn from Scripture, the medical and social sciences can fill out our perceptions of a complex human reality. Effective pastoral ministry presupposes a sound understanding of the relevant biblical principles and the relevant empirical data; neither can be neglected.

Synthetic Phase ("Process")

In the synthetic phase the goal is to process the various informational inputs and reach a conclusion. This involves reading the sources, taking notes, and mentally organizing the material. The information must not only be read and filed, but more importantly, assessed and weighed. What arguments and considerations are emerging as the central and compelling ones? What lines of evidence and argumentation bear upon these key foci? In the case being discussed here, the question of the "cultural conditioning" of biblical revelation will emerge as a fundamental issue. Are the biblical pronouncements on homosexuality limited by their time and culture? How are they to be related to modern research in the social sciences? What elements of biblical revelation are appropriate foundations for secular legislation?

This process of weighing the evidence and the arguments is of all the phases of research perhaps the most difficult to reduce to an explicit and formalized procedure. There is a sizable "unprogramed" and intuitive element at work here. In weighing the data, it is frequently helpful to discuss the problem with someone else. The very act of verbalizing our thinking process in someone else's presence can give focus and definition to our work. Often a question raised by a friendly listener can be more productive than hours of solitary reading in generating new insights and new directions to pursue.

Once we have reached a tentative conclusion, it is especially helpful to attempt to express the essence of that conclusion in a brief sentence or two. We haven't completely understood the impact of the research until such a concise statement can be made. (Of course we may conclude that at this stage our information is inadequate and the whole matter is inconclusive.) This phase is parallel to the attempt to clearly focus key terms, concepts, and distinctions at the beginning of the research process.

Finally, in this synthetic phase, it is worthwhile to attempt to *generalize* our conclusions. What do our conclusions imply for other related areas, for example, Christian attitudes toward legislation concerning divorce, abortion, or Sabbath observance? This attempt to generalize will often have the effect of making us more consciously aware of the *open-ended* nature of groundbreaking research. Answers in one area should generate new questions and avenues of investigation in other areas. In this case, for example, the whole question of the relationship of theology and psychology as alternative ways of understanding human nature could be a significant "spin-off" of the research.

Expressive Phase ("Output")

The expressive phase is concerned with the communication of the results of our theological research, in either written or oral form, to the parties concerned. This might be in the form of a sermon, a lesson, a pastoral conversation, or a term paper. For any of these forms, it is quite helpful to prepare a clear outline of the results we wish to communicate. The discipline of outlining is not only an aid in effective communication, but also a help in selecting the most relevant pieces of information from the extensive body of material processed during our research and reflection.

If the final product is to be in written form, several tools should be available to us: a good unabridged dictionary, and a copy of *A Manual For Writers of Term Papers, Theses, and Dissertations* by Kate L. Turabian. The content of our communication is more significant than its form, but *effective* communication is hindered by poor grammar, spelling, and syntax. If you have deficiencies in this area, have someone proofread your final draft before typing the finished copy. This practice can be beneficial even when your grasp of the mechanics of written expression is satisfactory. On matters of style and syntax, *Elements of Style* by Strunk and White is quite helpful.

Finally, as part of this expressive phase, it is wise to consider the *pastoral dimensions* of the process of communicating the results. What is the state of understanding and maturity of the people to whom I will be communicating? What are the human dynamics of the situation that could impede the understanding of what I am trying to say? What forms of language will be most helpful to the individuals and groups involved? Such questions appropriately bring our theological reflections back to the point at which they originated, namely, the actual life situations of those involved in the work of ministry.

2

Brief Glossary of Theological Terms

An asterisk preceding a term indicates the definition of that term is included in the glossary.

Allegory: A mode of speech, generally narrative in form, in which persons, places, objects, and events are held to have symbolic meanings. Unlike a *type*, an allegory is not necessarily based on a historical person or event; in distinction from a *parable*, an allegory is not limited to a single main point. Allegorical interpretations of Scripture were common in the patristic and medieval periods but have been largely rejected by the Reformers and modern Protestants.

Analogia Entis: A doctrine found in medieval and scholastic theology, and defended vigorously by Thomas Aquinas. According to this doctrine, from the being of the universe we may reason back analogically and proportionately to God.

The doctrine of the analogy of being was strongly attacked by Karl Barth in *Church Dogmatics*, where he insisted that God cannot be known from the creation, but only in the revelation in Jesus Christ.

While Barth's position serves as a corrective to an autonomous natural theology, it does not appear to do justice to the degree of moral accountability presupposed on the basis of general revelation in such texts as Romans 1:18-23.

Anthropology: The part of the theological system devoted to the study of the origins, nature, and destiny of man. Since the nineteenth century, anthropology has become an increasingly prominent focus of theological reflection. In formulating the doctrine of man, systematic theology attempts to integrate the data of the social sciences within a framework based on divine revelation.

Anthropomorphism: The attribution of human characteristics to God. In biblical usage physical characteristics are occasionally predicated of God in a metaphorical sense (e.g., Gen. 3:8; Num. 11:23; Ps. 33:18). Personal characteristics such as intellect, feelings, and will are predicated of God in a real though qualified sense. Anthropomorphic usage in Scripture reflects the fact that human relationships derive ultimately from the creative will of the personal God (cf. Eph. 3:15) who created man in his own image and likeness (Gen. 1:26).

Antinomy: In theology, one of a pair of apparently conflicting statements, each of which possesses claims to validity. Notable examples of biblical antinomies include the divine and human natures in the one person of Jesus Christ, and the concurrence of divine sovereignty and human responsibility in the process of salvation. Biblical antinomies arise when the divine reality intersects with the human, and point to the inability of human reason to exhaustively comprehend the nature and actions of God.

Apologetics: The intellectual defense of the Christian faith. Topics traditionally dealt with in apologetics include the relationship of faith and reason; proofs for the existence of God; creation and evolution; the problem of evil; miracles and natural law; evidence for the resurrection of Christ; the inspiration of Scripture. In contemporary evangelical circles discussions of methodology in apologetics usually involve the differences between the schools commonly known as *evidentialism and *presuppositionalism.

Arminianism: A theological movement initiated by Jacobus Arminius (1560-1609) of the Netherlands in reaction to the Calvinistic understanding of predestination, divine grace, and salvation. The followers of Arminius, called Arminians or Remonstrants, further developed the views of Arminius. The tenets of later Arminianism emphasize, but are not limited to, the following five doctrines: man's depravity resulting from the fall is not total; God's election is not unconditional but is based on foreseen faith; Christ died for the sins of all, not just the sins of the elect; the grace of God in the gospel calling to conversion can be resisted; a truly regenerate person may fall from grace and lose his salvation altogether. The Calvinistic party in the Netherlands rejected those propositions at the Synod of Dort (1618-1619).

Attributes of God: The perfections of the divine Being. The *incommunicable* attributes, emphasizing the absolute distinction between the Creator and the creature, include aseity or self-existence, immutability, eternity, omnipresence, and simplicity. The *communicable* attributes, reflected in a limited degree in the creature, include omniscience, wisdom, goodness, love, mercy, patience, holiness, righteousness, truth, and omnipotence. The divine attributes mutually qualify one another and may be said to be identical with the divine nature or essence.

Bibliology: The part of the theological system devoted to the doctrine of Scripture. Important concepts usually treated include authority, revelation, inspiration, illumination, and inerrancy.

The doctrine of Scripture was not systematically articulated in the early church and patristic era. Since the rise of modern biblical criticism, it has become one of the primary foci of theological reflection among evangelicals.

Calvinism: The theological tradition associated with John Calvin (1509-1564) and his later followers. The Synod of Dort (1618-1619) affirmed "Five Points" which are commonly held to be key tenets of classical Calvinism: total depravity or the total inability of man to contribute to his own salvation; unconditional election, that is, election apart from any foreseen faith; limited or definite atonement; irresistible or effectual grace; perseverance of the saints.

Christology: The part of the theological system dealing with the person and work of Christ. Ecclesiastical reflection on the person of Christ achieved classical expression in the Creed of Chalcedon (451). Reflection on the nature of the work of Christ (atonement) has exhibited greater variation across the centuries. Evangelicals stress the priestly and substitutionary dimensions of the biblical understanding of the work of Christ.

In any theological system Christology will play a central role, inasmuch as the understanding of the person and work of Christ is determinative for the understanding of salvation and the Christian life.

Coherence Theory of Truth: The theory which holds that truth consists in coherence with other statements known to be true. The coherence theory has been held by rationalist metaphysicians such as Gottfried Leibniz, Benedict Spinoza, Georg Hegel, and F. H. Bradley, and more recently, by the logical positivists Otto Neurath and Carl Hempel. While the coherence theory is quite appropriate in *a priori* disciplines such as mathematics and logic, it is less so in empirical disciplines such as history and the natural sciences.

Common Grace: The general benevolence of God toward the creature, benevolence which restrains the destructive consequences of sin, and enables the unregenerate to act in external conformity to the moral law and to exhibit creativity in works of culture (cf. Gen. 1:28; Matt. 5:45; Rom. 2:14). The concept of common grace helps the Christian to better appreciate the positive contributions and partial insights of non-Christian peoples.

Contextualization: A theological term prominent in recent discussions in missiology and liberation theology. Contextualization refers to the process through which the substance of biblical revelation is interpreted and applied in terms of the categories and thought forms of those who are receiving the message. Systematic theology, like counseling and homiletics, seeks to be context-specific in its application of biblical truth.

Correlation, Method of: A method of structuring the theological system articulated by Paul Tillich in the first volume of his *Systematic Theology.* Existential "questions" from the human situation are correlated with "answers" drawn from divine revelation. The method in itself is a sound one, as long as divine revelation, rather than the human situation, controls the nature of the theological agenda.

Correspondence Theory of Truth: The theory which holds that truth consists in some form of correspondence between belief and the actual state of affairs in the world. During the twentieth century, due to the influence of the modern scientific outlook, it has often been held that this correspondence must in all cases be capable of empirical verification. While Christian faith is deeply rooted in history and in the structures of the spatiotemporal world, the correspondence of the Christian position as a whole to ultimate reality will only be verified eschatologically, that is, by the return of Christ at the end of history.

Cosmological Argument: An argument for God's existence proceeding from the existence of the world to God as the world's sufficient cause. Its defenders have included Plato, Aristotle, Aquinas, René Descartes, Gottfried Leibniz, John Locke, Charles Hodge, Norman Geisler, and most Roman Catholic theologians; among its critics have been David Hume, Immanuel Kant, J. S. Mill, Bertrand Russell, and Gordon Clark. While philosophers are divided on the question of whether the argument makes belief in God's existence *logically inescapable*, Romans 1:18-21 indicates that, given God's general revelation in nature, disbelief in God is *morally inexcusable.*

Covenant Theology: A stream in the Reformed theological tradition emphasizing covenants in relation to God's dealings with humanity and the unity of the Old and New Testaments. Covenant theology was developed by the Continental Reformed theologians Olevianus (1536-1587) and Ursinus (1534-1583) and by William Ames (1576-1633), an English Puritan, and given a central place in the work of the nineteenth-century Princeton theologians Charles and A. A. Hodge.

Critical Philosophy: A term most often associated with the philosophy of Immanuel Kant, especially with regard to the epistemological doctrines presented in *The Critique of Pure Reason* (1781). Kant argued that we cannot know reality as it is in itself, but only as it appears to us, mediated through the categories of the human mind. Kant also denied the validity of the traditional proofs for the existence of God, holding that the concept of God must be understood as a postulate of moral experience.

Cultural Conditioning: A term used to designate the influence of the cultural context on the outward form of biblical revelation. The study of hermeneutics addresses the task of distinguishing the normative content of biblical revelation and its cultural form. See also *historicism.

Demythologizing: A method of interpreting the New Testament (German: *Entmythologisierung*) proposed by the German theologian and biblical scholar Rudolf Bultmann (1884-1976). The "mythological" cosmology and categories of the New Testament are to be translated into the categories of existentialist philosophy, especially as developed by the philosopher Martin Heidegger (1889-1976), in order to make the Christian message more understandable to modern men steeped in the world view of the natural sciences. Bultmann's attempt to communicate the Christian message effectively in the modern age is severely defective in that it virtually eliminates the supernatural element in historic biblical Christianity, thus fundamentally altering the nature of the message itself.

Dispensationalism: A system of biblical interpretation associated with J. N. Darby (1800-1882) and his followers and popularized through the notes of the Scofield Reference Bible. Dispensationalists distinguish seven periods in biblical history: Innocence (before the fall); Conscience (from the fall to Noah); Human Government (from Noah to Abraham); Promise (from Abraham to Moses); Law (from Moses to Christ); Grace (the church age); the Kingdom (the millennium). Dispensationalists draw sharp distinctions between God's purposes for Israel and for the church and emphasize literal fulfillments of Old Testament prophecies.

Dort, Synod of: An assembly of the Dutch Reformed Church convened in Dort (Dordrecht) in response to the Arminian controversy. The synod, meeting from November 1618 to May 1619, affirmed the authority of the Belgic Confession, the Heidelberg Catechism, and the "Five Points" of Calvinism. See *Calvinism.

Ecclesiology: The part of the theological system dealing with the doctrine of the church. Topics usually treated include the nature of the church; attributes of the church; forms of government and ministry; sacraments; and the mission of the church.

Although in the past evangelicals have sometimes tended to ignore ecclesiology, in the latter part of the twentieth century questions concerning the nature of the church and its ministry and mission have been moving to the forefront of contemporary theological reflection.

Election: The divine action whereby certain persons are chosen by God for special privilege and blessing; preeminently, God's choice of some for eternal salvation. According to the Arminian tradition, God's election is conditioned upon foreseen faith; according to the Reformed tradition, God's election is unconditional—faith being the consequence rather than the condition of divine election.

Epistemology: The branch of philosophy concerned with the possibility, nature, and conditions of human knowledge. Modern philosophy has been dominated by epistemological concerns, reflecting the impact of the work of René Descartes (1596-1650) and Immanuel Kant (1724-1804). Empirical epistemologies take the data of the senses to be the primary means of acquiring knowledge. Rationalistic epistemologies stress the perception of clear and distinct ideas by the human mind, often taking mathematics and logic as paradigms. In Christian theology, fideistic epistemologies hold that valid knowledge of God is acquired when the believer by faith appropriates the witness of the Holy Spirit to divine revelation. As in soteriology, so in epistemology: knowledge of God becomes a possibility for man only at God's initiative, by grace through faith.

Eschatology: The doctrine of the "last things": the intermediate state; the return of Christ; the general resurrection; the last judgment; and the eternal state.

It is now increasingly recognized that eschatology is not merely the last in a series of theological loci, but in a very real sense, the horizon of all New Testament theology. In the New Testament, Christian existence is lived within the tension of the "already"-"not yet" structure of the kingdom of God, which is both a present reality and a future hope.

Esthetics: The branch of philosophy concerned with the nature and criteria of beauty. A number of issues dealt with in esthetics, for example, the nature of metaphor and symbol and their relation to human cognitive and affective states, are particularly relevant to the concerns of theology and hermeneutics.

American evangelicals in this century have not, for the most part, shown great interest in esthetic questions. Theologically, this may be reflective of an inadequate grasp of the biblical doctrine of creation, and an almost exclusive concentration on the cognitive rather than the affective dimensions of divine revelation.

Ethics: The study of the principles of right conduct. Ethical systems can be broadly classified as either deontological or teleological. In deontological systems the basic ethical motif is obedience to laws or norms, understood either as laws of reason (Immanuel Kant) or as laws of divine revelation (Judaism; Islam; conservative Protestantism). In teleological systems, the basic ethical motif is the pursuit of some human good; for example, happiness (Aristotle); pleasure (Epicurus); the vision of God (Aquinas); the greatest good of the greatest number (J. S. Mill, Jeremy Bentham) or the will to power (Friedrich Neitzsche).

Evidentialism: A term designating a theory of apologetics which holds that the truth claims of Christianity must be verified by appealing to historical evidences available to believer and unbeliever alike, rather than by appeal to revelational starting points. Proponents of an evidential apologetic today include John Warwick Montgomery, Clark Pinnock, and Josh McDowell.

Existentialism: A philosophical orientation characteristic of such modern thinkers as Sören Kierkegaard, Martin Heidegger, Jean-Paul Sartre, Albert Camus, Karl Jaspers, and Gabriel Marcel. Existentialists hold that neither traditional metaphysics nor the natural sciences are adequate for understanding the deepest issues of human life. In the twentieth century theologians such as Karl Barth, Emil Brunner, Dietrich Bonhoeffer, Rudolf Bultmann, and Paul Tillich have been influenced in various degrees by the existentialist tradition.

Fideism: A term designating a theory of apologetics and biblical authority which holds that the ultimate ground for accepting the claims of Scripture is the testimony of the Holy Spirit to the Word of God, received by faith in the believer's experience. While not minimizing the role of reason and historical evidences, fideists hold that these elements, apart from the Spirit's witness, can produce only probable judgments, and not the certainty of faith. Advocates of this position include Calvin and the Westminster divines, and today, J. I. Packer and Donald Bloesch.

Form Criticism: An approach in biblical studies pioneered by Hermann Gunkel in relation to the Old Testament narratives of Genesis, and by Martin Dibelius and Rudolf Bultmann in relation to the Gospels. Form critics attempt to understand the literary subunits of the text in terms of the process of their oral transmission and usage in the life of the community. Some presuppositions of the more radical form-critics are in tension with an evangelical view of the authority of Scripture, especially where the creative contributions of the community are so emphasized as to endanger the essential continuity between history and theology in the biblical text.

Hermeneutics: In theology, the study of the principles and presuppositions of biblical exegesis. In the narrower sense of *biblical* hermeneutics, the primary concern is to recover the meaning which the text had for its original recipients. In the broader sense of *theological* hermeneutics, the concern is to bridge the chronological and cultural distance between the text and contemporary context by relating the text to the thought forms and categories of the modern world. In the latter sense, systematic theology functions as a "hermeneutical bridge" between the Bible and the contemporary world. See also *New Hermeneutic.

Historicism: A philosophical outlook which became prominent during the nineteenth century, reflecting the influence of Hegelianism, the historical studies of the Bible, and the theory of evolution. As defined by Ernst Troeltsch (d. 1923), historicism is the tendency to view all forms of knowledge and experience in the context of historical change.

For the evangelical, the relativistic implications of historicism are mitigated by the constancies of human nature and by the core of divine revelation which is normative in all ages.

Illumination: The witness of the Holy Spirit to the Word of God which enables the believer to understand its saving content (cf. Ps. 119:27, 73; Matt. 16:17; Acts 16:14; I Cor. 2:12-13).

Inerrancy: A consequence of divine inspiration, preserving the writers of Scripture from all error in their teaching. There are several views held by evangelicals concerning the scope of inerrancy. One view holds that inerrancy is predicated only of biblical teaching concerning faith and practice. Another view holds that inerrancy also extends to matters of scientific and historical detail. Both views are agreed that sound biblical interpretation takes into account such factors as authorial intent, literary genre, colloquial expressions, approximations, and the like. Synonym: infallibility.

Infralapsarian: In relation to the doctrine of election, the view which holds that election follows the fall in the logical order of the divine decrees. According to infralapsarians, the logical order of the divine decrees is (1) the decree to create; (2) the decree to permit the fall; (3) the decree to elect some to be saved. This view appears to be in accord with the biblical correlation of divine salvation and human sin, and with the divine attributes of justice, holiness, and wisdom. Antonym: *supralapsarian.

Inspiration: A term referring to the divine origin of the Scriptures, through the Holy Spirit's influence upon the human authors. The doctrine of inspiration presupposes God's providential supervision over the entire process of the formation of the canon, so that the original revelation was recorded and transmitted in ways consistent with the divine intention. Evangelicals hold that inspiration is *plenary*, extending to all parts of the canonical books, and *verbal*, extending to the very words of the text, and not merely the ideas contained therein. The terms *confluent* and *organic* are used to denote a view of inspiration which recognizes the instrumentality of the human writer's personality, as opposed to "mechanical" or "dictation" views.

Liberation Theology: A contemporary theological movement which interprets salvation and the mission of the church primarily as the changing of oppressive socio-economic and political structures, rather than as redemption from individual guilt and sin. Heavily indebted to the social analysis of Karl Marx, liberation theology parallels many of the features of the social gospel in America earlier in this century. Contemporary advocates of liberation theology include James Cone, Frederick Herzog, Letty

Russell, Rosemary Ruether, Gustavo Gutiérrez, José Míguez Bonino, Rubem Alves, and Hugo Assmann.

Logic: The branch of philosophy concerned with the rules of valid inference and reasoning. Inductive reasoning proceeds from particulars to general principles; deductive reasoning proceeds from general principles to particular conclusions.

The study of logic was first systematized by Aristotle and further developed by European and Arabian thinkers during the Middle Ages. Since the nineteenth century, philosophers have tended to focus their attention on highly abstract systems of symbolic and mathematical logic.

In Christian theology, human logic, operating under the authority of Scripture and the guidance of the Holy Spirit, has the legitimate tasks of defending biblical truth from skeptical attacks, and showing the coherence of the various elements of the organism of Christian truth. While human logic can assist in preserving revealed mysteries such as the Trinity and the incarnation from heretical distortion, human logic in and of itself can never fully comprehend them. Human logic points to the mysteries, and guards them, but can never claim to fully possess or control them.

Logical Positivism: A philosophical position advocated during the 1930s by A. J. Ayer and others which held that all meaningful statements must be capable of empirical verification. According to this view religious and metaphysical statements are neither true nor false, but in the strict sense, meaningless. Critics of this view pointed out that the positivist criterion of empirical verifiability was not itself capable of empirical verification, but was based on an implicit judgment of the truth of metaphysical materialism.

Lutheranism: The ecclesiastical and theological tradition associated with the Protestant Reformer Martin Luther (1483-1546) and his followers. Two of the cardinal tenets of the Lutheran tradition are expressed in the phrases *sola fide* and *sola scriptura*—justification by faith alone, and Scripture alone as the supreme authority for faith and life. The church is understood not as a hierarchical structure, but as a spiritual community, a "priesthood of all believers." The Lutheran view of the Lord's Supper, commonly known as *consubstantiation*, holds that the body and blood of Christ are present to the believer "in, with, and under" the elements of bread and wine.

Marxism: The philosophy associated with the life and thought of Karl Marx (1818-1883), also known as dialectical materialism. In Marxist thought the laws, values, customs, and beliefs of any society are a reflection of, and to a great extent determined by, the more basic socioeconomic realities of that society, especially the nature of the ownership of the means of production. Human thought is determined by the social structure, and not vice versa.

Marxism is important not only as a powerful competitor to Christianity, but also in terms of its influence in contemporary theology, especially among liberation theologians. In such theologies a Marxist analysis of society functions as a hermeneutical key for interpreting and applying the Christian message. See *liberation theology.

Metaphysics: The branch of philosophy concerned with the nature and structures of being or ultimate reality. Traditionally, metaphysics has addressed such issues as the nature of existence, properties, and events; the relation between particulars and universals, individuals and classes; the nature of change and causation; and the nature of mind, matter, space, and time.

Since the time of Kant (1724-1804), metaphysics as traditionally conceived has been in disfavor in Protestant theology. More recently, there has been a revival of interest in metaphysics among process theologians who have attempted to restate Christian faith in terms of the metaphysical vision of Alfred North Whitehead.

Basic to a biblical outlook on metaphysics is the fundamental distinction between the Creator and the creation. The objectively existing and knowable structures of the created world reflect the creative power, wisdom, and will of the Triune God, as mediated through Jesus Christ the Logos, who is the mediator between the uncreated God and the created order.

Natural Theology: A term used to designate that which can be known of God apart from special revelation. Roman Catholicism, reflecting the position of Thomas Aquinas, holds that the existence of God can be proven by reason alone. Modern Protestant theology, reflecting Immanuel Kant's, David Hume's, and Karl Barth's philosophical and theological criticisms of the traditional theistic proofs, has tended to deny the validity of natural theology. Recent process theologians such as John B. Cobb, Jr., Schubert Ogden, and David Griffin have, however, argued for its validity. Evangelical Protestants are divided on the issue. See *evidentialism, *presuppositionalism, *fideism.

Neoorthodoxy: A twentieth-century theological movement most prominently associated with the work of Karl Barth and Emil Brunner. Reacting to both nineteenth-century liberalism and seventeenth-century confessional orthodoxies, neoorthodoxy stressed the transcendence of God, revelation as primarily a personal encounter with God rather than the communication of propositional information, the priority of divine grace and faith in the knowledge of God, and the reality of human sin. After assuming a dominant position between the First and Second World Wars, neoorthodoxy declined in influence during the later 1950s and 1960s.

New Hermeneutic: A post-Bultmannian development in

Protestant theology associated with the work of Ernst Fuchs, Gerhard Ebeling, Hans-Georg Gadamer, Robert W. Funk, and James M. Robinson. By drawing on the later philosophical writings of Martin Heidegger, proponents of the New Hermeneutic are attempting to transcend the limitations of a purely historical-critical approach to exegesis and to develop a theory of interpretation which will translate the historical meaning into the contemporary situation. As presently formulated, the New Hermeneutic still bears the marks of its Bultmannian heritage, limiting the arena of the divine-human encounter to human inwardness, rather than allowing for the possibility of God's real action in observable spatiotemporal history.

Noetic Effects of Sin: The darkening of the human mind by sin, so that a special influence of divine grace is needed for understanding and obeying biblical truth (cf. I Cor. 1:18; 2:12-14; II Cor. 4:4; Eph. 4:17-18).

Ontological Argument: An argument for the existence of God proposed by Anselm (1033-1109). Defining God as "that than which none greater can be conceived," Anselm argued that such a definition logically implies God's necessary existence. The argument was criticized by Aquinas and Immanuel Kant, and defended by René Descartes, Georg Hegel, and more recently by Charles Hartshorne. Evaluations of the validity of the argument turn on judgments concerning the possibility of establishing the relationship between the mind and external reality by the powers of reason alone. At the very least, the argument can be seen as an articulation of the nature of God as self-existent, infinite, and eternal, as presented to human experience in God's own self-revelation.

Pantheism: The belief that the substance of God and the substance of the world are in some sense identical. Such views have characterized much of classical Hinduism, and, in the West, can be seen in the philosophical positions of Benedict Spinoza and Georg Hegel.

This is to be distinguished from *panentheism*, the view which holds that the being of God includes the being of the universe, but at the same time transcends it. Panentheism is characteristic of contemporary process theology.

Person(s): In trinitarian usage, the term used to refer to the distinct yet interpenetrating centers of individuality in the divine life: Father, Son, and Holy Spirit. The terms *persona* (Lat.) and *hypostasis* (Gr.) refer to the eternal distinctions within the divine life; the terms *substantia* (Lat.) and *ousia* (Gr.) to the eternal ground of unity.

Point of Contact: A term made famous by a debate between Emil Brunner and Karl Barth during the 1930s. Is there a point of contact for the gospel in the natural man? Brunner argued that the sense of guilt constitutes such a point of contact. Barth, on the contrary, argued that the only point of contact is the faith created by the preaching of the Word of God (*Church Dogmatics*, I/1, p. 273).

Reformed theologians have tended to see in the existence of common grace (cf. Matt. 5:45; Acts 14:17) and the image of God such a point of contact or common ground for doing Christian apologetics.

Pragmatism: One of the most influential philosophies in America during the first quarter of the twentieth century. Most often associated with the work of Charles S. Peirce (1839-1914), William James (1842-1910), and John Dewey (1859-1952), pragmatism stressed the practical consequences of an idea as a measure of its truth. William James could speak of truth as the "cash value" of an idea. While rightly stressing the relationship of truth to the practical concerns of life, pragmatism is inadequate in and of itself for choosing the ultimate goals or ends—as opposed to methods and means—of human existence in time and eternity.

Predestination: The eternal foreordination by God of all events, including the salvation of certain individuals (cf.

Acts 2:23; 4:28; Rom. 8:29-30; Eph. 1:5, 11). *Election can thus be understood as a subcategory of predestination. From Latin *praedestinare*, the Vulgate translation of Greek *proorizo*, "foreordain."

Presuppositionalism: A term designating a theory of apologetics which holds that biblical revelation is the necessary presupposition of any coherent system of truth. According to Gordon Clark, all true statements are either explicitly stated in Scripture, or must follow from scriptural statements through sound logical inference. According to Cornelius Van Til, the existence of the Triune God and the infallible authority of Scripture are the necessary presuppositions for knowing the truth of any fact whatsoever.

Process Theology: A contemporary theological movement based on a view of reality in which process, change, and evolution are just as fundamental as substance, permanence, and stability. God, in a continuous and creative relationship of involvement with the world, is himself understood to be undergoing a process of self-development and growth. Basic to process theology is the metaphysical system of Alfred North Whitehead's *Process and Reality*. Contemporary advocates of process theology include Charles Hartshorne, John B. Cobb, Jr., Schubert Ogden, and David Griffin.

Redaction Criticism: A recent trend in New Testament scholarship in which the evangelists are seen not as mere compilers of the tradition, but as theologians who creatively shaped their material in the light of their understanding of Christ and the situations of the churches they were addressing. Redaction critics are concerned to recover the distinctive perspectives of the Gospel writers. Evangelicals can affirm this concern without endorsing the tendency of the more radical critics to separate theology from factual history in the Gospel accounts.

Revelation: The process by which God acts in history,

makes himself personally present to his people, and communicates to them his saving will, purposes, and claims upon their lives. Revelation thus encompasses God's deeds, God's presence, and God's word; it is both "personal" and "propositional" in nature.

Revelation refers to the original deed, self-presentation, or communication of God; *inspiration to its divinely superintended recording in Scripture; *illumination to its application to the contemporary believer through the ministry of the Holy Spirit.

Soteriology: The branch of theology which deals with salvation or redemption. Traditionally, soteriology is divided into objective soteriology and subjective soteriology. Objective soteriology is concerned with the active and passive obedience of Christ: Christ's active obedience to the law of God as the second Adam; his satisfaction of divine justice through his substitutionary and atoning death on the cross. Subjective soteriology, or the application of the work of redemption by the Holy Spirit, deals with calling, regeneration, faith, repentance, conversion, justification, sanctification, perseverance, and glorification.

In recent theologies there have been noticeable tendencies to reinterpret salvation in anthropocentric and socioeconomic categories. See *liberation theology.

Supralapsarian: In relation to the doctrine of election, the view which holds that election precedes the fall in the logical order of the divine decrees. According to supralapsarians, the logical order of the decrees is: (1) the decree to elect some foreseen as created but not yet fallen; (2) the decree to create; (3) the decree to permit the fall. Antonym: *infralapsarian.

Teleological Argument: The argument that the existence of order or design in the world implies the existence of an intelligent designer, that is, God. The argument has been defended by Aquinas and William Paley (1743-1805), criticized by Immanuel Kant and David Hume, and in this century defended in various forms by R. E. D. Clark and F. R. Tennant. Insofar as it presupposes the principle of causality, this argument can be understood as a special case of the *cosmological argument.

Theology: In the broader sense, the subject matter of the theological system as a whole; in the narrower sense, the doctrine of God. Theology proper deals with the existence, knowability, attributes, and triune nature of God. In some traditions, the doctrines of the decrees and divine predestination are treated in connection with theology proper.

Typology: A method of biblical interpretation in which the persons and events of the Old Testament are understood to foreshadow the deeper spiritual meanings of New Testament revelation: for example, Jonah and the resurrection of Christ (Matt. 12:40); the crossing of the Red Sea and Christian baptism (I Cor. 10:1-6). The possibility of valid typological meanings in the Old Testament cannot be excluded without invalidating the insights of the New Testament writers themselves. See *allegory.

Wesleyanism: The ecclesiastical and theological tradition associated with John Wesley (1703-1791) and his followers. As an expression of the Protestant Reformation, historic Wesleyanism holds to the supreme authority of Scripture, the Trinity, the deity of Christ, the universality of sin, and other classical Christian doctrines. Special emphases of the Wesleyan tradition include a stress on personal religious experience and the new birth; the conviction that Christ died for all, and not for the elect only; the doctrine of preliminary or prevenient grace, which to some extent counteracts the effects of original sin; and the teaching of Christian perfection or entire sanctification, which holds that the believer can in this life experience God's grace to such an extent that the heart is emptied of all sin and filled with a pure love for God and the neighbor.

Will of God: Theological discussions distinguish the decretive, preceptive, and permissive wills of God. The decretive will determines whatsoever comes to pass, and is normally known only after the fact. The preceptive will reveals God's norms for moral conduct, and may be either obeyed or disobeyed by moral agents. The permissive will refers to those actions which, though not in accord with divine precepts, are permitted by God and ultimately are redirected to serve redemptive purposes (Gen. 50:20).

3

Brief Guide to Modern Theologians

The following brief sketches are not intended to be a comprehensive guide to either the biographies or the theologies of the figures listed. This guide is intended to give the beginning student some initial orientation to the lives and positions of theologians whose names are likely to be encountered in lectures and reading assignments.

Representative works are listed for each theologian. In the case of translated works, the date cited is that of the commonly available English translation. An asterisk preceding a name indicates a biographical sketch of that person is included in this chapter.

Barth, Karl *(1886-1968)*. Swiss neoorthodox theologian. Born in Basel; studied at Berne, Berlin, Tübingen, and Marburg; held pastorates in Geneva and Safenwil; taught at universities of Göttingen, Münster, Bonn, and Basel; a leader in the resistance of the German Confessing Church against Nazism and a leading contributor to the drafting of the Barmen Declaration (1934).

Barth's theology can be understood as a forceful reaction against the optimistic and man-centered orientation of the nineteenth-century theology of *Schleiermacher and the followers of Hegel. Barth stressed the transcendence of God over man and his culture and religion; the necessity of divine revelation and the futility of natural theology; the finitude and sinfulness of man and the priority of divine grace; the need to rediscover the insights of the Bible and the Protestant Reformers.

Contrasted with Protestant liberalism, Barth's theology represented a profound recovery of biblical themes. The defects of this approach include a tendency to separate revelation from empirically verifiable historical events, and a separation of the "Word of God" and Scripture—with the consequence that the cognitive basis of divine revelation is eroded.

Anselm: Fides quaerens intellectum, 1962; *Church Dogmatics*, 1936-1969; *Natural Theology*, 1946; *Protestant Thought: From Rousseau to Ritschl*, 1959.

Bavinck, Herman (1854-1921). Dutch Reformed theologian. Born in Hogeveen in the Netherlands, the son of a pastor. Bavinck was educated at the Theological School of the Christian Reformed Church and the University of Leiden, and taught theology at the Theological School in Kampen and at the Free University of Amsterdam, where he succeeded Abraham Kuyper.

Bavinck's major work, the four-volume *Gereformeerde Dogmatiek (Reformed Dogmatics)*, is characterized by its close adherence to the data of Scripture, its concern for the historical development of doctrine, and a synthetic style of reasoning which frequently attempts to bring various viewpoints closer together.

Bavinck was also active in the ecclesiastical affairs of his day and gave significant leadership to the Christian school movement in the Netherlands.

Gereformeerde Dogmatiek, 1906-1911; *The Doctrine of*

God, 1951 (tr. of vol. 2 of *Ger. Dog.*); *Our Reasonable Faith*, 1956; *The Philosophy of Revelation*, 1953.

Berkhof, Louis *(1873-1957)*. American Reformed theologian. Born in the Netherlands, Berkhof was educated at Calvin Seminary and Princeton. He taught for many years at Calvin Seminary, and also served as its president. Standing in the tradition of Abraham Kuyper and Herman Bavinck, Berkhof was considered a representative spokesman for orthodox Calvinism in the United States.

History of Christian Doctrines, 1937; *Principles of Biblical Interpretation*, 1950; *Systematic Theology*, 1941.

Berkouwer, G. C. *(1903-   )*. Dutch Reformed theologian. Berkouwer was educated at the Free University of Amsterdam, and after serving a number of years in the pastorate, was called back to the university to teach dogmatics, a position previously held by Abraham Kuyper, Herman Bavinck, and Valentinus Hepp.

With the publication of his multivolume *Studies in Dogmatics* Berkouwer has established himself as one of the leading evangelical theologians of Europe. In his writings he has stressed the integral relation of theological reflection and the living faith of the church. He has expressed reservations about the concept of inerrancy as it was articulated in the Hodge-Warfield tradition.

The Second Vatican Council and the New Catholicism, 1965; *Studies in Dogmatics*, 14 vols., 1952-1976; *The Triumph of Grace in the Theology of Karl Barth*, 1956.

Bloesch, Donald *(1928-   )*. American evangelical theologian. Born in Bremen, Indiana, Bloesch was educated at Elmhurst College, Chicago Theological Seminary, and the University of Chicago. He is presently professor of theology at Dubuque Theological Seminary in Dubuque, Iowa.

Standing within the broader Reformed tradition, Bloesch has attempted to mediate some of the past disputes between Calvinism and Arminianism, and between

Calvinism and Lutheranism. His writings display both a critical and an appreciative relationship to the neoorthodox and Roman Catholic theological traditions.

Essentials of Evangelical Theology, 2 vols., 1978-1979; *The Evangelical Renaissance*, 1973; *The Ground of Certainty*, 1971; *The Reform of the Church*, 1970.

Bonhoeffer, Dietrich *(1906-1945)*. German Lutheran theologian. Born in Breslau, Germany, and educated at Tübingen, Berlin, and Union Theological Seminary, Bonhoeffer was active in the German Confessing Church's resistance to Nazism. Implicated in a plot to assassinate Hitler, he was arrested in 1943 and executed in 1945.

In its general orientation Bonhoeffer's theology has considerable affinity with the neoorthodox movement associated with Karl Barth. Bonhoeffer became well-known in English-speaking circles through his criticisms of "cheap grace" in *The Cost of Discipleship*, through his emphasis on Christian community in *Life Together*, and through the fragmentary passages of his posthumous *Letters and Papers from Prison*, which later became a major source of inspiration for the theologies of secularity in the 1960s.

The Cost of Discipleship, 1960; *Creation and Fall*, 1959; *Ethics*, 1955; *Letters and Papers from Prison*, 1967; *Life Together*, 1954; *Temptation*, 1955.

Brunner, Emil *(1889-1966)*. Swiss neoorthodox theologian. Brunner, who taught theology for many years at the University of Zürich, shared many of the theological concerns of Karl Barth, but differed sharply with Barth on the question of natural theology. Unlike Barth, Brunner held that some valid knowledge of God is available to man in creation, apart from special revelation. Brunner made extensive use of the "I-Thou" philosophy of Martin Buber, and stressed the "personal" rather than the propositional or cognitive aspects of divine revelation. Brunner, more so than Barth, believed that it is part of the theologian's task to enter into sympathetic dialogue with secular thinkers and representatives of non-Christian religions.

The Divine Imperative, 1947; *Dogmatics*, 3 vols., 1950-1962; *The Mediator*, 1947; *The Misunderstanding of the Church*, 1953; *Revelation and Reason*, 1946.

Bultmann, Rudolf *(1884-1976)*.   German New Testament scholar and neoorthodox theologian. Bultmann was educated at Marburg, Tübingen, and Berlin, and taught New Testament studies at the universities of Breslau, Giessen, and Marburg. He was instrumental in the development of form-critical studies of the Gospels, stressing the faith of the early church rather than historical events *per se* as the key to the theological significance of the documents. Bultmann is perhaps best remembered for his program of "demythologizing," in which he insisted that the entire structure of the New Testament is "mythological" (e.g., a three-storied universe, angels, demons, miracles), and consequently needs to be translated into the categories of existentialist philosophy in order to be understandable to modern man.

Bultmann's reinterpretation of the miraculous element in the New Testament effectively denies the omnipotence of God, and has affinity with a deistic conception of God's relationship to the world. Bultmann's later disciples have tended to react against his sharp separation of faith and history in studies of the historical Jesus.

Existence and Faith, 1960; *Faith and Understanding*, 1969; *The History of the Synoptic Tradition*, 1963; *Jesus Christ and Mythology*, 1958; *Theology of the New Testament*, 1951, 1955.

Carnell, E. J. *(1919-1967)*.   American evangelical theologian and apologist. Born in Antigo, Wisconsin, Carnell was educated at Wheaton College, Westminster Theological Seminary, Harvard, and Boston University. From 1945 to 1948 he taught at Gordon College and Divinity School.

In 1948 he joined the faculty of Fuller Theological Seminary, and served as its president from 1954 to 1959.

Carnell was one of the chief leaders in the intellectual reawakening of American evangelicalism after World War II. In his apologetic methodology he attempted to combine elements of the evidential and presuppositional schools.

The Case for Orthodox Theology, 1959; *Introduction to Christian Apologetics*, 1948; *The Theology of Reinhold Niebuhr*, 1951.

Clark, Gordon H. *(1902-   ).* American evangelical philosopher and apologist. Born in Philadelphia, Clark studied at the University of Pennsylvania, Heidelberg, and the Sorbonne. He has taught at the University of Pennsylvania, Reformed Episcopal Seminary, Wheaton College, Butler University, and Covenant College.

Clark is known in American evangelical circles for his penetrating discussions of ancient and modern philosophy, his staunch defense of Calvinistic orthodoxy and biblical inerrancy, his emphasis on the cognitive aspect of divine revelation, and his epistemology which holds that all valid truths are either explicitly stated in the Scriptures or are logically deducible from Scripture.

A Christian View of Men and Things, 1952; *From Thales to Dewey*, 1956; *Religion, Reason, and Revelation*, 1961.

Cone, James *(1938-   ).* American liberation theologian. Cone, who is presently Charles A. Briggs Professor of Systematic Theology at Union Theological Seminary in New York, is perhaps the most prominent of American black theologians. According to Cone, who in his theological work draws significantly from Marxist insights for his understanding of the sociological dimensions of the Christian faith, the central message of the gospel is liberation from the various forms of human oppression, as understood within the context of the black experience in America.

Black Theology and Black Power, 1969; *A Black Theology*

of Liberation, 1970; *God of the Oppressed*, 1975; *The Spirituals and the Blues: An Interpretation*, 1972.

Geisler, Norman *(1932-   )*. American evangelical apologist and philosopher of religion. Born in Warren, Michigan, Geisler was educated at Wheaton College and Graduate School, Detroit Bible College, and Loyola University. He has taught at Detroit Bible College, Trinity College (Ill.), Trinity Evangelical Divinity School, and is presently professor of theology at Dallas Theological Seminary.

Noted for his advocacy of the value of Thomistic philosophy for evangelical apologetics, Geisler has recently articulated a sophisticated defense of the validity of the cosmological argument for the existence of God.

Christian Apologetics, 1976; *Ethics: Alternatives and Issues*, 1971; *Philosophy of Religion*, 1974.

Gerstner, John *(1914-   )*. American Reformed church historian and theologian. Born in Tampa, Florida, Gerstner studied at Westminster Theological Seminary and Harvard. After serving as a pastor for five years, he joined the faculty at Pittsburgh-Xenia Seminary in 1950. Since the merger of Pittsburgh-Xenia and Western Seminary he has served on the faculty of Pittsburgh Theological Seminary as professor of church history.

Gerstner is noted in American evangelical circles for his staunch Calvinism, his defense of biblical inerrancy, his opposition to the ordination of women as teaching and ruling elders, and his advocacy of a rational-evidential apologetic in the tradition of Charles Hodge and Benjamin B. Warfield.

A Bible Inerrancy Primer, 1965; *A Predestination Primer*, 1960; *Reasons for Faith*, 1960; *The Theology of the Major Sects*, 1960.

Harnack, Adolf von *(1851-1930)*. German church historian and theologian. Harnack, one of the outstanding patristic scholars of his generation, taught at the universities of Leipzig, Giessen, Marburg, and Berlin. In his *History of Dogma* he examined the development of Christian doctrine from a theological standpoint which considered the use of Greek metaphysical categories in the early creeds to be a distortion of the primitive Christian faith. In his famous lectures at the University of Berlin during the 1899-1900 academic year, later published as *What Is Christianity?*, he gave a moralistic interpretation of the Christian faith, holding that the ideas of the fatherhood of God, the brotherhood of man, and the Sermon on the Mount as an ethical ideal constitute the essence of the faith. As a proponent of exacting historical studies, and of a theological standpoint characterized by a moralistic and antimetaphysical bent, Harnack epitomized many of the crucial emphases of nineteenth-century liberal theology.

History of Dogma, 7 vols., 1894-1899; *What Is Christianity?*, 1901.

Henry, Carl F. H. *(1913-   )*. American evangelical theologian. Born in New York City, Henry was educated at Wheaton College, Northern Baptist Theological Seminary, and Boston University. He has taught at Northern Baptist Seminary, Fuller Seminary, Wheaton College, Gordon Divinity School, Trinity Evangelical Divinity School, Eastern Baptist Seminary, and has served as editor of *Christianity Today.*

A prolific writer standing within the Reformed tradition, Henry played a leading role in the renewal of evangelical scholarship after World War II. His writings have argued for the rational defensibility of the Christian faith and the importance of the cognitive element in divine revelation.

Christian Personal Ethics, 1957; *God, Revelation, and Authority*, 4 vols. so far, 1976-   ; *The Uneasy Conscience of Modern Fundamentalism*, 1948.

Hodge, Charles *(1797-1878)*. American Presbyterian theologian. Born in Philadelphia, and educated at Princeton College and Seminary, Hodge was a leading theologian in America for much of the nineteenth century. He taught for more than fifty years at Princeton Seminary, and exerted great influence in the affairs of the Presbyterian church and American ecclesiastical life generally. He was noted as a vigorous defender of orthodox Calvinism and the verbal inspiration and infallibility of Scripture.

Commentary on the Epistle to the Romans, 1836; *Constitutional History of the Presbyterian Church*, 1839-1840; *Systematic Theology*, 3 vols., 1871-1872.

Küng, Hans *(1928-   )*. German Roman Catholic theologian. Küng, professor of dogmatic and ecumenical theology at the University of Tübingen, has been known in Catholic and Protestant circles for his interest in church renewal, ecumenical relations, and restating the faith for contemporary man. More recently he has been disciplined by the magisterium for his attack on papal infallibility and his denial of the literal truth of the preexistence of Christ, the virgin birth, and the deity of Christ as understood in the Formula of Chalcedon. In these latter matters, Küng's positions seem reminiscent of the positions of nineteenth-century Protestant liberalism and the demythologizing program of Rudolf Bultmann.

The Church, 1967; *Infallible? An Inquiry*, 1971; *Justification: The Doctrine of Karl Barth and a Catholic Reflection*, 1964; *On Being a Christian*, 1976; *Structures of the Church*, 1964.

Machen, J. Gresham *(1881-1937)*. American Presbyterian New Testament scholar and apologist. Born in Baltimore, Machen was educated at Johns Hopkins, Princeton University and Seminary, Marburg, and Göttingen. During the years 1906-1929 he taught New Testament at

Princeton Seminary, resigning in 1929 due to the liberal realignment of the seminary. He was a principal founder of Westminster Theological Seminary and what is now the Orthodox Presbyterian Church. From 1929 to 1937 he served as president and professor of New Testament at Westminster. Machen was one of the primary intellectual leaders of the conservatives during the modernist-fundamentalist controversies of the 1920s and 1930s.

Christianity and Liberalism, 1923; *The Origin of Paul's Religion*, 1927; *The Virgin Birth of Christ*, 1930.

Moltmann, Jürgen *(1926-   )*. German Protestant theologian. Since 1967 Moltmann has been professor of systematic theology at the University of Tübingen. He became a prominent theological figure in 1964 with the publication of *Theology of Hope* which emphasized eschatology and the categories of hope and promise as central elements in Christian theology. More recently Moltmann's interests have focused on "political theology," stressing the Christian message as a message bringing release from dehumanizing socioeconomic and political forces. In the process, the biblical call for individual repentance and regeneration has been somewhat neglected.

The Church in the Power of the Spirit, 1977; *The Crucified God*, 1974; *Religion, Revolution, and the Future*, 1969; *Theology of Hope*, 1967.

Niebuhr, Reinhold *(1892-1971)*. American Protestant theologian. After studying at Elmhurst College, Eden Theological Seminary, and Yale Divinity School, Niebuhr spent thirteen years in the pastorate in Detroit, and then accepted an invitation in 1928 to teach ethics at Union Theological Seminary in New York. Niebuhr shared many of the tenets of neoorthodoxy (e.g., in the areas of biblical authority and in a symbolic understanding of creation and fall), but emphasized more strongly than Barth the need for Christian involvement in social and political reform.

The doctrine of man was a central focus of Niebuhr's work. In his discussions of human nature, original sin, and the ambiguities of history and of the exercise of power, Niebuhr incisively criticized the more optimistic views of man which had characterized older Protestant liberalism and the social gospel.

Christianity and Power Politics, 1940; *Moral Man and Immoral Society,* 1932; *The Nature and Destiny of Man,* 2 vols., 1946.

Orr, James *(1844-1913).* Scottish evangelical theologian and apologist. Born in Glasgow, Orr was educated at the University of Glasgow, and taught at the United Presbyterian Theological College of Scotland and at the United Free Church College in Glasgow.

He was known on both sides of the Atlantic as a capable and articulate defender of evangelical positions.

The Christian View of God and the World, 1897; *God's Image in Man,* 1905; *The Progress of Dogma,* 1901; *The Virgin Birth of Christ,* 1915.

Packer, James I. *(1926-   ).* British evangelical theologian. Born in Gloucestershire, England, Packer was educated at Oxford, taking degrees in classics, philosophy, and theology. He has taught at Tyndale Hall and Trinity College, Bristol, and during the 1960s was warden of Latimer House, an evangelical study center at Oxford. He has been a visiting professor at Westminster, Fuller, Trinity, and Gordon-Conwell seminaries, and is presently on the faculty of Regent College in Vancouver.

Standing in the Reformed and evangelical stream of the Anglican tradition, Packer draws much inspiration for his theological work from the English Puritans. In his defense of the inspiration and infallibility of Scripture he has stressed Scripture's self-attesting authority and the witness of the Holy Spirit rather than evidential considerations.

Evangelism and the Sovereignty of God, 1961; "*Fundamentalism*" *and the Word of God*, 1958; *Knowing God*, 1973.

Pannenberg, Wolfhart (1928-   ). German Protestant theologian. Since the 1960s Pannenberg has emerged as one of the most prominent European Protestant theologians. Educated at the universities of Basel, Heidelberg, and Göttingen, he has been professor of systematic theology at the University of Mainz and, since 1968, professor at the University of Munich.

In certain respects Pannenberg's theology can be seen as a criticism of the theologies of Barth and Bultmann. In Pannenberg's view, divine revelation is open to investigation through the rational and historical methods shared with other scholarly disciplines. The resurrection of Christ is, in principle, open to confirmation through historical research. Theology must be in continual dialogue with other disciplines in a common search for truth and reality.

Pannenberg's positions are a healthy corrective to the tendencies in neoorthodox and existentialist theologies to separate revelation from reason and history. At the same time, there seems to be an insufficient grasp of the bearing of the noetic effects of sin and the witness of the Holy Spirit in relationship to the understanding of divine revelation.

Jesus—God and Man, 1968; *Theology and the Kingdom of God*, 1969; *Theology and the Philosophy of Science*, 1976.

Pieper, Franz (1852-1931). American Lutheran theologian. Born in Germany, Pieper was educated at Northwestern (Watertown, Wis.) and Concordia Seminary at St. Louis. He taught at Concordia from 1878 to 1931, and served as its president from 1887 to 1931.

One of the best-known theologians of the Missouri Synod Lutheran Church, Pieper gave special emphasis in

his dogmatics to the doctrines of grace and inspiration.
Christian Dogmatics, 4 vols., 1950-1957.

Rahner, Karl *(1904-   ).* German Roman Catholic theologian. Born in Breslau, Rahner entered the Society of Jesus in 1922, was ordained in 1932, and after a period of study with Martin Heidegger, completed his doctoral studies in 1936. Since 1948 he has taught dogmatic theology at the universities of Innsbruck, Munich, and Münster.

Rahner, one of the most innovative and prolific of living Roman Catholic theologians, has written on a wide range of systematic, philosophical, and pastoral issues. His theological outlook, frequently characterized as "transcendental Thomism," attempts a synthesis of classical Thomism and the philosophical tradition of German idealism, variously represented by Immanuel Kant, Georg Hegel, and Martin Heidegger. Evangelical Protestants would question a fundamental characteristic of Rahner's theological method, that is, his starting point in a philosophical understanding of man rather than the divine revelation in Scripture. Rahner's conclusions are often controversial, for example, his view of the incarnation combining aspects of classical and process theology, his concept of the "anonymous Christian" and salvation through non-Christian religions, and his belief in the inescapability of theological pluralism within the church itself.

Encyclopedia of Theology (ed.), 1975; *Foundations of Christian Faith,* 1978; *Hearers of the Word,* 1969; *Spirit in the World,* 1968; *Theological Investigations,* 16 vols., 1961-

Rauschenbusch, Walter *(1861-1918).* American Protestant theologian and social reformer. The son of a German-born Baptist minister, Rauschenbusch was educated in America and Germany, graduated from Rochester Theological Seminary, and served as pastor of a working-class

German Baptist church in New York City, where he became concerned to relate the Christian faith to the social needs of his day. In 1897 Rauschenbusch was called to teach at Rochester Theological Seminary.

As a leader in the social-gospel movement, Rauschenbusch found inspiration in the ideal of the kingdom of God stressed in the liberal tradition of Ritschl and Harnack. The kingdom of God was to be progressively realized in history through the reign of love in human affairs, exemplified in the life and teachings of Jesus of Nazareth, the inaugurator of a new humanity. While Rauschenbusch discerned the reality of the corporate structures of evil, his theology tended to underestimate the radical nature of indwelling sin in the individual, and the need for personal regeneration. The social-gospel movement was eclipsed by the rise of neoorthodoxy in the 1930s, but more recently many of its concerns have found expression in various liberation theologies and in a renewed concern among American evangelicals for social demonstration of the gospel.

Christianity and the Social Crisis, 1907; *Christianizing the Social Order*, 1912; *A Theology for the Social Gospel*, 1917.

Schleiermacher, Friedrich (1768-1834). German liberal Protestant theologian. Born in Breslau, Schleiermacher spent most of his life in Berlin as a preacher and professor of theology. Often known as the "father of liberal theology," he argued that the essential character of the Christian religion is not to be found in doctrinal truths or in a system of ethics, but rather in a personal experience of divine realities, in religious feeling. Religion itself is a "feeling of absolute dependence," a God-consciousness most perfectly realized in the consciousness of Jesus of Nazareth. Christian doctrines are attempts to give verbal expression to the fundamental experiences of piety.

In reacting to the rationalistic philosophy and orthodox

theology of his own day, Schleiermacher developed a theological outlook which, while having the merit of stressing the importance of personal religious experience, devalued the importance of doctrinal truth and the role of Scripture as an objective norm for Christian faith and practice.

The Christian Faith, 1822; *On Religion: Speeches to Its Cultured Despisers*, 1799.

Thielicke, Helmut (1908-   ). German Lutheran theologian; professor emeritus of systematic theology, the University at Hamburg, Germany. Known in English-speaking circles as a gifted preacher and ethicist, Thielicke's theological position has recently been comprehensively set forth in his systematic theology, *The Evangelical Faith*. Working from a standpoint influenced both by the Lutheran and neoorthodox traditions, Thielicke has attempted to delineate a theology which is neither merely a "conservative" repetition of the Christian tradition nor a "modern" transmutation of its content into categories acceptable to the "modern mind."

Christ and the Meaning of Life, 1962; *Encounter with Spurgeon*, 1963; *The Evangelical Faith*, 1974-   ; *Theological Ethics*, 1966.

Tillich, Paul (1886-1965).   German Protestant theologian. Tillich, the son of a German Lutheran pastor, was educated at the universities of Berlin, Breslau, and Halle, and taught theology and philosophy at Berlin, Marburg, Dresden, Leipzig, and Frankfurt. He emigrated to America in 1933 and taught at Union Theological Seminary in New York, Harvard, and the University of Chicago.

Tillich's philosophical theology, heavily influenced by existentialism and German idealism, employs a "method of correlation" in which questions from the human situation are related to answers from divine revelation. Jesus Christ is understood as the bearer of the "New Being," who overcomes man's estrangement, anxiety, and guilt.

Tillich offers highly symbolic interpretations of Christian doctrines such as creation, fall, and resurrection, and makes little direct use of Scripture in developing his theological system. He was one of the most influential theologians in America during the 1950s and 1960s.

The Courage to Be, 1952; *Dynamics of Faith*, 1957; *Systematic Theology*, 1951-1963; *Theology of Culture*, 1959.

Van Til, Cornelius *(1895-)*. American Reformed apologist. Born in the Netherlands, Van Til came to the United States with his family in 1905. He was educated at Calvin College, Princeton Theological Seminary, and Princeton University. After one year (1928-1929) of teaching at Princeton Seminary, he joined the newly-formed faculty of Westminster Theological Seminary, where he taught apologetics for more than forty years.

Known as a vigorous defender of a presuppositional approach in apologetics, Van Til insists that the infallible truth of Scripture and the existence of the Triune God are the necessary presuppositions for the knowledge of any truth whatsoever.

A Christian Theory of Knowledge, 1969; *Common Grace*, 1947; *The Defense of the Faith*, 1963; *The New Modernism*, 1946.

Warfield, Benjamin B. *(1851-1921)*. American Presbyterian theologian. Born near Lexington, Kentucky, Warfield was educated at Princeton University and Seminary and at the University of Leipzig. From 1878 to 1887 he taught at Western Theological Seminary in Pittsburgh, and then accepted a call to teach didactic and polemical theology at Princeton Theological Seminary, where he succeeded A. A. Hodge, the son of Charles Hodge.

Warfield was perhaps the most learned conservative scholar of his day, being proficient in theology, patristics, and New Testament exegesis. He was committed to the Calvinism of the Westminster Confession of Faith and the inerrancy of Scripture. His writings continue to be influential in American conservative circles today.

Counterfeit Miracles, 1918; *Inspiration and Authority of the Bible*, 1948; *The Lord of Glory*, 1907; *The Plan of Salvation*, 1915.

Whitehead, Alfred North *(1861-1947).* Anglo-American mathematician and philosopher. Whitehead, who began his career as a mathematician in England, moved to the United States and taught philosophy for thirteen years at Harvard. He developed a process metaphysics in which change and development are as fundamental to the nature of reality as permanence. In Whitehead's metaphysics God's nature is "bi-polar," having both a "primordial" (or eternal) aspect and a "consequent" aspect which is affected by the change and temporality of the world. Whitehead's views have been a major source for contemporary process theologians such as John B. Cobb, Jr., Charles Hartshorne, Schubert Ogden, and Norman Pittenger.

Adventure of Ideas, 1933; *Process and Reality*, 1929; *Science and the Modern World*, 1925.

4

Truth:
Philosophical and
Theological Issues

Philosophical Issues

Pragmatic Theory of Truth

Pragmatism, one of the most influential philosophies in America during the first quarter of the twentieth century, gave rise to a distinctive concept of the nature of truth. Most often associated with the work of Charles S. Peirce (1839-1914), William James (1842-1910), and John Dewey (1859-1952), pragmatism stressed the practical consequences of an idea as a measure of its truth. In the words of William James, truth is that which "proves to be good in the way of belief"; it is the "expedient in the way of our thinking." James could even speak of the truth of ideas as their "cash value." According to John Dewey, the hypothesis that works is the true one. Truth is that which is instrumental to an active reorganization of a given environment, or which helps to remove some specific trouble or perplexity.

A pragmatic theory of truth thus conceived is paralleled by the earlier conception of Karl Marx (1818-1883), in which truth is not so much a theory about reality, as a power or program for altering reality. The truth of an idea is manifested in *praxis*, in its effectiveness in altering man's socioeconomic environment.

Such pragmatic theories of truth have had a continuing appeal to the practically-oriented American temperament, and have the advantage of keeping theoretical reflection related to practical concerns. Nevertheless, pragmatic theories all share a basic limitation, namely, that any criterion of "expediency" or "usefulness" cannot in itself give an adequate answer to the question, "Useful in relation to what ultimate end?" Answering the question of the ultimate end of human existence requires a metaphysical or revelational starting point, rather than a merely pragmatic one.

Coherence Theory of Truth

The coherence theory of truth is characteristic of the rationalist metaphysical systems of Gottfried Leibniz (1646-1716), Benedict Spinoza (1632-1677), Georg Hegel (1770-1831), and F. H. Bradley (1846-1924). More recently, this theory has been advocated by the logical positivists Otto Neurath (1882-1945) and Carl Hempel (1905-   ), who were greatly influenced by the models of pure mathematics and theoretical physics. According to the coherence theory, a statement is true if it coheres with a system of statements already known to be true, or with a system of statements deduced from self-evident axioms. Proponents of this theory hold that particular facts or statements have meaning only when seen as parts of an organic and self-consistent whole. The coherence theory of truth has the merit of stressing the essential unity and relatedness of all truth, but it also has a number of significant weaknesses.

For a given set of facts, it is possible to propose any number of coherent explanations, each of which might appear to be internally consistent. The criterion of coherence alone is not sufficient for choosing among the competing explanations. The test of coherence with a system of statements already known or believed to be true may also prove inadequate when dealing with dramatic new facts or discoveries which are not easily assimilated within standard frames of reference, for example, the discovery of radioactivity and its impact on classical physics. Revolutionary discoveries, rather than being accredited within the older frames of reference, often become the basis for constructing new and more comprehensive ones.

Features of the coherence theory of truth may be found in the apologetic systems of the twentieth-century Reformed theologians Gordon H. Clark (1902-   ) and Cornelius Van Til (1895-   ). According to Clark, the one fully coherent system of truth is based on the axiom, "The Bible is the Word of God." The predicate "true" can be applied only to the statements contained in the Bible, or to statements which can be logically deduced from the Bible. This position has the advantage of assigning to Scripture an absolute epistemological priority in Christian theology and apologetics, but it has the grave defect of leaving no place for sense experience in the knowing process. It is difficult to see how true statements such as "giraffes are taller than zebras" or "Peking is the capital of China" are deducible from statements found in Scripture.

According to Van Til, the actual existence of the Triune God and the infallible authority of the Bible are the necessary presuppositions of the intelligibility of any fact in the world. Particular facts are known to be true only as part of a complete system, and, according to Van Til, the only system which provides coherence is the one based on these basic Christian presuppositions of the existence of the Triune God and the infallible authority of Scripture.

Strictly speaking, then, the unbeliever has no grounds for knowing that any of his beliefs are true. While this view has the merit of stressing the ultimate relatedness of all truth to the basic premises of biblical revelation, it does not appear to do adequate justice to the fact that those who hold radically different systems, for example, Muslims, Christian Scientists, Marxists, and Skinnerians, all believe that their systems give coherent and intelligible interpretations of human experience and reality as a whole. For the Christian, of course, the existence of the Triune God and the infallible authority of Scripture are the necessary starting points for a comprehensive system of truth, but this is seen to be the case only after conversion, and through the eyes of faith.

Correspondence Theory of Truth

From ancient times to the present, some form of the correspondence theory has tended to be the dominant model for understanding the nature of truth. Aquinas, drawing on an earlier Neoplatonic tradition, defined truth as "the adequation of things and the intellect." In this century Bertrand Russell has argued that "truth consists in some form of correspondence between belief and fact." If a given statement corresponds to the actual state of affairs in the world, that statement is said to be true. Such a formulation would appear to be in keeping with our usual common-sense understandings of the nature of truth.

While evangelical Christians are in general agreement that the truth of Christianity does consist in its correspondence to the structures of objective reality, there is not unanimity on the exact nature of that correspondence, or on the means by which that correspondence is to be verified. Contemporary evangelical apologists such as John Warwick Montgomery and Clark Pinnock stress the role of historical evidences in verifying the truth claims of Christianity. Such an "evidential" approach clearly has strong biblical support (e.g., John 5:36; 10:25; I Cor. 15:17). At the same time, arguments based on historical evidence, apart from the inner witness of the Holy Spirit, at best lead to a high degree of probability, not to the certainty of faith. Proponents of Van Til's apologetic approach also argue that a historical "fact" can be properly understood only as part of a larger framework of meaning provided by the biblical view of reality. The empty tomb can be seen either as an inexplicable quirk of nature, or as evidence for the deity of Christ, depending on one's total frame of reference. Spiritually significant "facts" can be perceived only by those who are willing to submit to their claims upon personal life (John 7:17). In order to see the facts of the kingdom of God, to recognize them for what they are, one must be born again (John 3:3), and become a recipient of the Holy Spirit, who heals our blindness to the truths of the Christian faith (cf. I Cor. 2:14).

The pragmatic, coherence, and correspondence theories of truth complement one another in the Christian's attempts to give an account of the truth value of faith. The believer finds the claims of Christ verified in personal experience, in the unfolding of a comprehensive and coherent view of reality, and in the correspondence of the biblical data to the facts of history. In the last analysis, however, the believer's certitude rests on the inner testimony of the Holy Spirit to the Word of God, since certain challenges to faith—for example, the presence of radical evil in the world—cannot be totally overcome by philosophical appeals to common sense and evidences. The believer looks forward to an ultimate *eschatological* verification of the faith, when, at the return of Christ, all doubts will be banished, and the truth of the Christian faith will be a massive and undeniable reality to unbeliever and believer alike.

Theological Issues

Revelation: "Personal" or "Propositional"?

In the twentieth century there has been a continuing debate about the nature of divine revelation and truth in theology. Is divine revelation primarily "personal" or "propositional" in nature? Those influenced by neoorthodox theologians such as William Temple (1881-1944), John Baillie (1886-1960), and Emil Brunner (1889-1966) have tended to argue that divine revelation is primarily a personal encounter with God in Christ, rather than the transmission of information about God. This point of view, representing in part a reaction against the older Roman Catholic view of faith as intellectual assent to propositions taught by the church, and the stress in seventeenth-century Protestant orthodoxy on precise doctrinal formulation, reflects the philosophical influence of existentialist thinkers such as Sören Kierkegaard (1813-1855) and Martin Buber (1878-1965). In response to such emphases, theological conservatives have tended to stress the propositional or cognitive dimensions of divine revelation. As is often the case in theological controversies, both positions witness to important dimensions of the truth. The neo-orthodox position rightfully focused attention on the dynamic and personal characteristics of God's revelation to man. The conservative emphasis on the cognitive dimension of the revelatory event is an essential biblical corrective, however, since without a divine *interpretation* of the revelatory event, one is left with a contentless experience or a barren mysticism. A proper view of Christian truth distinguishes the personal and propositional elements, but does not separate them.

"Orthodoxy" or "Orthopraxis"?

In recent years a number of Latin American liberation

theologians have argued that truth consists more in right action (*orthopraxis*) than in right belief (*orthodoxy*). According to the Brazilian theologian Rubem Alves (1933-   ), "Truth is the name given by the historical community to those actions which were, are and will be effective for the liberation of man." This understanding of truth reflects the Marxist conception in which ideas are understood primarily as instruments for social change, rather than as disinterested reflections on the structures of reality. Liberation theologians quote with approval the famous dictum of Marx: "The philosophers have only *interpreted* the world in various ways; the point is, to *change* it."

Such a view of truth can function as a needed corrective to rarefied forms of thinking which ignore the concrete needs of existing human beings and the problems arising from unjust social structures. The biblical revelation does indeed point to the integral relation existing between the genuine knowledge of God and obedience to God, an obedience which implies concern for the poor and oppressed. There is a real danger, however, that such views will substitute secular models of human liberation for the biblical one. The truth of God does indeed liberate human beings oppressed by sin and its consequences, but not necessarily with either the means or the immediacy that human wisdom might expect.

Truth: Absolute or Culturally Relative?

During the modern era a number of philosophical and cultural currents have combined to call into question for many the very idea of absolute and unchanging truth, whether in the Bible or elsewhere. Many studies in cross-cultural anthropology and comparative religions tended to stress the diversity of belief systems held by the various cultural groups under consideration. The philosophy of Karl Marx and the discipline known as the sociology of knowledge stress the influence of the social environment on both the form and content of all human thinking, including religious thought. The historical-critical method of studying the Scriptures, especially as it was practiced during the nineteenth century, at times so emphasized the details of the original historical context of the biblical text that the abiding religious content was displaced or obscured. These factors all tended to erode belief in abiding and eternal truths, and helped to foster the mood of relativism which is so characteristic of contemporary thought.

It is the case, of course, that God reveals truth through the specific languages, cultures, and historical contexts of the biblical writers. Responsible biblical interpretation demands that the reader of Scripture give the most careful attention to the original setting of the writings in order to discern the intentions and purposes of the sacred writers. Only through such foundational study can the significance of the text for the contemporary situation be appropriated. While in practice it may at times be difficult to neatly distinguish abiding principles and the specific cultural forms in which they are applied by the biblical writers, in principle this can and must be done. The instruction, for example, that women should not pray in church without a veil (I Cor. 11:5) should be seen as a culturally specific way of applying the more universal principle of I Corinthians 14:40, that in the church all things should be done decently and in order.

The universal and abiding character of biblical truth is rooted in the basic continuities of human nature, in God's unchanging character, and in God's sovereign control of all the processes of history and culture. The Bible speaks to man as he has always existed in the sight of God, as one who is made in the divine image, has fallen into sin, and is subject to the universal conditions of anxiety, guilt, fear, and loneliness. The God of Scripture is not the god of one culture or ethnic group, but the Creator of heaven and earth, the author of the laws of nature, the architect of the cosmic environment in which all men live. His character is eternal and unchanging. The sovereign God who speaks in Scripture is not the captive of the cultural forms which are the channels of divine revelation. The Word of God in its sovereignty and freedom efficaciously accomplishes the divine purpose (Isa. 55:11) through the instrumentality of human culture. "The grass withers, the flower fades; but the word of our God will stand for ever" (Isa. 40:8, RSV).

5

Bibliography:
Introduction to Theology

The literature of theology is enormous. The following bibliography has been prepared for a first course in theology with the beginning student especially in view. Works of particular value to the student have been indicated with an asterisk. In the case of translated works, the date of publication listed refers to more generally available reprints.

In preparing this work I have received helpful assistance from the bibliographic work of John Bollier, Roger Nicole, and Clark Pinnock, whose efforts are gratefully acknowledged.

Bibliographic Resources

The following include tools for locating journal articles and book reviews.

Adams, Charles J., ed. *A Reader's Guide to the Great Religions*. 2nd ed. New York: Free Press, 1965, 1977.
  Bibliographic guide to world religions; pp. 370-385 deal with Christian theology and philosophy.

*Bollier, John A. *The Literature of Theology: A Guide for Students and Pastors*. Philadelphia: Westminster Press, 1979.
  Concentrates on reference and bibliographic tools rather than on monographs.

Book Reviews of the Month. Fort Worth: Southwestern Baptist Theological Seminary, 1962 to date.
  Helpful for locating reviews of recently published books; for reviews of older works, see *Religion Index One*. No cumulative indices.

Catholic Periodical and Literature Index. Formerly *The Catholic Periodical Index*. Haverford, PA: Catholic Library Association, 1967/68 to date.
  Annual indexing of 133 Catholic periodicals; also includes book reviews.

Christian Periodical Index. Buffalo: Christian Librarian's Fellowship, 1956/60 to date.
  An index to subjects, authors, and reviews in some 59 popular and scholarly periodicals, mostly evangelical. Useful for locating articles not listed in *Religion Index One*.

"Elenchus Bibliographicus" in *Ephemerides Theologicae Lovanienses*. University of Louvain. Gembloux: Duculot, 1924 to date.
  A comprehensive bibliographic guide to theological literature in foreign languages and English prepared by Catholic scholars at the University of Louvain in Belgium. Includes books, reviews, journal articles, and pamphlets; no abstracts.

Montgomery, John W. *The Writing of Research Papers in Theology*. N.p., 1959.

Contains a list of "150 basic reference tools for the theological student," pp. 22-36.

The Philosopher's Index. Bowling Green, OH: Philosophy Documentation Center, 1967/68 to date; retrospective to 1940.
Comprehensive indexing of periodical literature in philosophy. Subjects and book reviews; author index with abstracts.

Religion Index One: Periodicals. Formerly *Index to Religious Periodical Literature.* Chicago: American Theological Library Association.
Subject-indexing for 210 theological and religious periodicals; includes author index with abstracts. An indispensable bibliographic tool.

Religion Index Two: Multi-Author Works.
Indexing by subject, author, and editor for multi-author books.

Religious and Theological Abstracts. Myerstown, PA: Religious and Theological Abstracts, 1958 to date.
Abstracts from some 150 journals covering biblical, theological, historical, practical, and sociological subjects. Author and subject indices for each volume.

*Wainwright, William J. *Philosophy of Religion: An Annotated Bibliography of Twentieth-Century Writings in English.* New York: Garland, 1978.
A valuable bibliographic tool for philosophical theology and apologetics. Abstracts of books and journal articles.

Dictionaries and Encyclopedias

Catholic

*Bouyer, Louis. *Dictionary of Theology.* Translated by Charles Underhill Quinn. Tournai, Belgium: Desclee, 1965.
Seeks "to give precise definitions of theological terms—and a concise synthesis of Catholic doctrine" (Foreword). Brief articles, with references to Scripture and ecclesiastical documents; no bibliography. A very helpful reference for traditional Catholic teaching.

The Catholic Encyclopedia. 15 vols. with index. New York: Encyclopedia Press, 1907-1912.

Dated, but still a valuable source for Catholic thought and scholarship in its historical development.

Davis, H. Francis; Williams, Aidan; Thomas, Ivo; and Crehan, Joseph, eds. *A Catholic Dictionary of Theology.* London: Thomas Nelson and Sons, 1962 ff. "A work projected with the approval of the Catholic hierarchy of England and Wales."

Comprehensive signed articles with bibliography. Citations from Scripture and church fathers.

New Catholic Encyclopedia. 17 vols. New York and Washington, DC: McGraw-Hill, 1967, 1974, 1979.

"An international work of reference on the teachings, history, organization, and activities of the Catholic Church, and on all institutions, religions, philosophies, and scientific and cultural developments affecting the Catholic Church from its beginning to the present" (Frontispiece). Prepared by an editorial staff at the Catholic University of America; a successor to the *Catholic Encyclopedia* of 1907-1912.

Parente, P.; Piolanti, A.; and Garofalo, S. *Dictionary of Dogmatic Theology.* Translated by E. Doranzo. Milwaukee: Bruce, 1951.

Brief definitions of theological terms, with bibliography. Contains a concise "Outline of the History of [Catholic] Dogmatic Theology."

*Rahner, Karl, ed. *Encyclopedia of Theology: The Concise Sacramentum Mundi.* New York: Seabury Press, 1975.

Some 400 articles, without bibliography, on theology, biblical studies, and related topics drawn from *Sacramentum Mundi* and other German reference works. A valuable and convenient reference tool for recent Catholic thought.

Rahner, Karl, and Vorgrimler, Herbert. *Theological Dictionary.* Edited by Cornelius Ernst. New York: Herder and Herder, 1965.

"The book is intended to provide brief explanations, in alphabetical order, of the most important concepts of modern Catholic dogmatic theology for readers who are prepared to make a certain intellectual effort" (Preface). Contemporary in approach; no bibliographies.

Rahner, Karl, et al. *Sacramentum Mundi: An Encyclopedia of Theology.* 6 vols. New York: Herder and Herder, 1968-1970.

A work characterized by concern for historical development and by "openness for the other Christian churches, the non-Christian religions, and for the world in general" (Preface). An important source for developments in post-Vatican II Catholicism.

Vacant, A., Mangenot, E., and Amann, E., eds. *Dictionnaire de Theologie Catholique.* 15 vols. Paris: Librairie Letouzey et Aue, 1930-1950.

A scholarly work in French on Catholic doctrine and ecclesiastical history.

Protestant

*Cross, F. L., ed. *The Oxford Dictionary of the Christian Church.* London: Oxford University Press, 1958.

Contains more than 6,000 concise articles, mostly by Anglican scholars, and nearly 4,500 brief bibliographies. "Its aim is to provide factual information on every aspect of Christianity, especially in its historical development." An invaluable reference tool.

Douglas, J. D., ed. *New International Dictionary of the Christian Church.* Grand Rapids: Zondervan, 1974, 1978.

Some 4,800 signed articles, mostly without bibliography, about persons, places, events, movements, denominations, and ideas in Christian history. Convenient for quick reference; conservative Protestant in orientation.

*Edwards, Paul, ed. *Encyclopedia of Philosophy.* 8 vols. New York: Macmillan, 1967.

Signed articles with bibliography covering the whole range of philosophy. Reflects the empirical and analytic tradition of Anglo-Saxon philosophy. Useful to both the novice and the specialist.

Halverson, Marvin, and Cohen, Arthur A., eds. *Handbook of Christian Theology.* Cleveland and New York: World, 1958.

Brief signed essays by American and European Protestant

scholars, with limited bibliography. Focuses on contemporary trends; reflects neoorthodox and liberal perspectives.

*Harrison, Everett F., ed. *Baker's Dictionary of Theology*. Grand Rapids: Baker, 1960.
A one-volume collection of brief signed articles, with bibliography, by conservative American and British scholars.

Harvey, Van A. *A Handbook of Theological Terms*. New York: Macmillan, 1964.
Quick reference for terms in systematic and philosophical theology. Cross-references; no bibliography.

Hastings, James, ed. *Encyclopedia of Religion and Ethics*. 12 vols. and index. Edinburgh: T. and T. Clark; New York: Charles Scribner's Sons, 1908-1927. Reprint, New York: Scribner, 1959.
Dated but still valuable. Lengthy articles with bibliography on Christian theology, philosophy, and world religions. Also includes material on anthropology, mythology, folklore, and sociology.

Jackson, S. M., ed. *The New Schaff-Herzog Encyclopedia of Religious Knowledge*. 12 vols. and index. New York: Funk and Wagnalls, 1908-1912. Reprint (13 vols.), Grand Rapids: Baker, 1949-1950.
A valuable work treating theology, Bible, church history, denominations, and missions. Bibliographies appended to each article.

Loetscher, Lefferts A., ed. *Twentieth Century Encyclopedia of Religious Knowledge*. 2 vols. Grand Rapids: Baker, 1955.
An extension and updating of *The New Schaff-Herzog Encyclopedia of Religious Knowledge*.

M'Clintock, John, and Strong, James, eds. *Cyclopaedia of Biblical, Theological, and Ecclesiastical Literature*. 12 vols. New York: Harper and Brothers, 1867-1887.
Dated, but still valuable for scholarly information on historical and doctrinal subjects.

*Richardson, Alan, ed. *A Dictionary of Christian Theology*. Philadelphia: Westminster, 1969.

Brief signed articles with bibliography, mostly by British scholars. "Emphasis is laid upon development of thought rather than biographical details or events of church history" (Preface). Especially helpful in areas of philosophy and contemporary developments in Christian thought.

Systematic Theologies

Aulén, Gustaf. *The Faith of the Christian Church.* Philadelphia: Fortress, 1960.
Swedish Lutheran. Attempts a middle course between fundamentalism and modernism.

Barth, Karl. *Church Dogmatics.* 4 vols. Edinburgh: Clark, 1936-1977.
The most voluminous work in twentieth-century theology.

Bavinck, Herman. *Our Reasonable Faith.* Grand Rapids: Eerdmans, 1956.
Dutch Reformed.

Berkhof, Hendrikus. *Christian Faith: An Introduction to the Study of the Faith.* Grand Rapids: Eerdmans, 1979.
Dutch Reformed. Fruitful interaction with contemporary thought; neoorthodox approach to Scripture.

Berkhof, Louis. *Systematic Theology.* Grand Rapids: Eerdmans, 1941, 1949.
Dutch Reformed. A standard text.

Berkouwer, G. C. *Studies in Dogmatics.* 14 vols. Grand Rapids: Eerdmans, 1952-1976.
The most extensive twentieth-century work in Dutch Reformed theology.

*Bloesch, Donald. *Essentials of Evangelical Theology.* 2 vols. San Francisco: Harper and Row, 1978-1979.
A recent expression of American evangelical theology. Generally Reformed in orientation, Bloesch makes use of positive insights from Roman Catholicism and Karl Barth.

*Brunner, Emil. *Dogmatics.* 3 vols. Philadelphia: Westminster, 1949-1960.
Swiss neoorthodox. Stresses "existential" rather than cognitive aspects of Christian faith; generally more readable than Barth.

*Buswell, J. O., Jr. *A Systematic Theology of the Christian Religion.* Grand Rapids: Zondervan, 1962.
American Calvinist. Attempts to keep theology and biblical exegesis closely tied.

*Calvin, John. *Institutes of the Christian Religion.* 2 vols. Edited by J. T. McNeill. *Library of Christian Classics.* Philadelphia: Westminster, 1960.
An all-time classic in Protestant theology. The McNeill edition has helpful annotations.

Chafer, L. S. *Systematic Theology.* 8 vols. Dallas: Dallas Seminary Press, 1947-1948.
American dispensationalist. Chafer taught for many years at Dallas Theological Seminary.

Cone, James H. *A Black Theology of Liberation.* Philadelphia and New York: J. B. Lippincott, 1970.
Interprets the gospel as essentially a message of liberation from oppression; written from the perspective of black experience in America.

Dabney, Robert L. *Lectures in Systematic Theology.* First published in 1878. Grand Rapids: Zondervan, 1972.
American Calvinist. Dabney was a leading nineteenth-century theologian of the Southern Presbyterian Church.

DeWolf, L. H. *A Theology of the Living Church.* New York: Harper, 1953.
Liberal Methodist.

Finney, Charles G. *Lectures on Systematic Theology.* Oberlin, OH: E. J. Goodrich, 1887.
American Arminian. Finney was a notable nineteenth-century evangelist and social reformer.

Hammond, T. C. *In Understanding Be Men.* Revised by D. F. Wright. Downers Grove, IL: Inter-Varsity, 1968.

Anglican evangelical. An introductory handbook of Christian doctrine suitable for church study classes.

Henry, Carl F. H., comp. *Fundamentals of the Faith*. Grand Rapids: Zondervan, 1969.

American evangelical. Previously published essays on theological themes by evangelical authors.

Hodge, A. A. *Outlines of Theology*. First published in 1860. Grand Rapids: Zondervan, 1972.

American Calvinist. Lectures by the son of Charles Hodge; still valuable.

*Hodge, Charles. *Systematic Theology*. 3 vols. First published in 1872. Grand Rapids: Eerdmans, 1975.

American Calvinist. The major work by the major theologian of the "Old Princeton" school.

Hoeksema, Herman. *Reformed Dogmatics*. Grand Rapids: Reformed Free Publishing Association, 1966.

Dutch Reformed. Hoeksema defends a supralapsarian view of election.

Kaufman, G. D. *Systematic Theology: A Historicist Perspective*. New York: Charles Scribner's Sons, 1968.

Liberal Mennonite. Kaufman teaches at Harvard Divinity School.

Kuyper, Abraham. *Principles of Sacred Theology*. First published in 1898. Grand Rapids: Eerdmans, 1954.

Dutch Calvinist. Discusses matters of prolegomena; helpful chapter on noetic effects of sin.

Lecerf, Auguste. *Introduction to Reformed Dogmatics*. London: Lutterworth, 1949.

French Reformed. Contains good discussion of principles of canonicity.

Litton, E. A. *Introduction to Dogmatic Theology*. London: Robert Scott, 1912.

Traditional Anglican. Written in the tradition of the Thirty-Nine Articles of the Church of England.

MacQuarrie, John. *Principles of Christian Theology*. New York: Charles Scribner's Sons, 1966.

Liberal Anglican. In his philosophical orientation MacQuarrie reflects the existentialist stance of Martin Heidegger.

Miley, John. *Systematic Theology.* 2 vols. New York: Eaton and Mains, 1892.

Wesleyan Arminian. Old, but still valuable.

Mueller, J. T. *Christian Dogmatics.* St. Louis: Concordia, 1934.

Missouri Synod Lutheran; largely a restatement of Franz Pieper's *Christliche Dogmatik.*

Mullins, E. Y. *The Christian Religion in Its Doctrinal Expression.* Philadelphia: Judson Press, 1917.

Mullins taught for many years at the Southern Baptist Theological Seminary in Louisville, Kentucky. Tries to steer a middle course between Calvinism and Arminianism; somewhat cursory treatment of inspiration of Scripture.

Pieper, Franz. *Christian Dogmatics.* 4 vols. St. Louis: Concordia, 1950-1957.

Missouri Synod Lutheran. Perhaps the best conservative Lutheran text in English.

Pohle, Joseph. *Dogmatic Theology.* 12 vols. St. Louis: Herder, 1911, 1946.

American Roman Catholic. A comprehensive treatment; pre-Vatican II perspective.

Pope, W. B. *A Compendium of Christian Theology.* 2nd ed. 3 vols. New York: Phillips and Hunt, n.d.

Nineteenth-century English Methodist; contains helpful discussions of the history of doctrine.

Prenter, Regin. *Creation and Redemption.* Philadelphia: Fortress, 1967.

Danish Lutheran. Neoorthodox in his view of revelation; stresses integral connection of creation and redemption.

Rahner, Karl. *Foundations of Christian Faith.* New York: Seabury, 1978.

Grounds theology within the horizon of human experience; draws philosophical resources from existentialism and phenomenology.

Russell, Letty M. *Human Liberation in a Feminist Perspective:*

A Theology. Philadelphia: Westminster, 1974.

Not a formal systematic theology, but deals with incarnation, salvation, and ecclesiology from a feminist perspective. Russell teaches at Yale Divinity School.

Schleiermacher, Friedrich. *The Christian Faith.* 2 vols. First published in 1821-1822. New York: Harper and Row, 1963.

Schleiermacher, the "father of liberal theology," held that theology is primarily an articulation of religious feeling and experience, rather than an expression of propositional truth or a system of ethics.

Shedd, W. G. T. *Dogmatic Theology.* 3 vols. New York: Scribner, 1888-1894.

American Presbyterian; Reformed. Comprehensive and still valuable. Shedd taught for many years at Union Theological Seminary of New York.

Stevens, W. W. *Doctrines of the Christian Religion.* Grand Rapids: Eerdmans, 1967.

Southern Baptist. Written primarily for college rather than seminary use.

Strong, A. H. *Systematic Theology.* First published in 1907. Valley Forge, PA: Judson, 1962.

American Baptist; Reformed. For many years a leading text in Baptist seminaries. Strong favored the concept of theistic evolution.

Thielicke, Helmut. *The Evangelical Faith.* 2 vols. Grand Rapids: Eerdmans, 1974, 1977.

German Lutheran; generally neoorthodox in orientation. An important contribution by a leading European theologian.

Tillich, Paul. *Systematic Theology.* 3 vols. Chicago: University of Chicago Press, 1951-1963.

German-American neoliberal. A comprehensive correlation of Christian revelation and human culture by one of the most influential figures in twentieth-century American theology. Philosophically indebted to Martin Heidegger and German idealism.

Warfield, B. B. *Biblical and Theological Studies.* Philadelphia: Presbyterian and Reformed, 1952.

A collection of doctrinal essays by a notable representative of the "Old Princeton" school.

*Wiley, H. Orton. *Christian Theology*. 3 vols. Kansas City, MO: Beacon Hill Press, 1960.
American; Church of the Nazarene. Perhaps the best recent text in the Arminian tradition.

Revelation

Baillie, John. *The Idea of Revelation in Recent Thought*. New York: Columbia University Press, 1956.
Neoorthodox.

Berkouwer, G. C. *General Revelation*. Grand Rapids: Eerdmans, 1955.
Reviews Barth-Brunner debate on natural theology and other issues related to the topic of general revelation.

Brunner, Emil. *Revelation and Reason*. Philadelphia: Westminster, 1946.
Stresses "personal" rather than "propositional" revelation; neoorthodox.

Downing, F. Gerald. *Has Christianity a Revelation?* London: SCM Press, 1964.
A trenchant analysis of the problems arising with the use of the concept of God's self-revelation in much recent theology, especially in neoorthodoxy.

*Henry, Carl F. H. *God, Revelation, and Authority*. Vols. 1-4. Waco, TX: Word Books, 1976, 1979.
A major evangelical contribution. Interacts extensively with contemporary thought; stresses cognitive element of revelation.

Latourellé, Rene. *Theology of Revelation*. Staten Island, NY: Alba House, 1966.
Roman Catholic.

*McDonald, H. D. *Ideas of Revelation: 1700-1860*. New York: Macmillan, 1959.
———. *Theories of Revelation: 1860-1960*. New York: Humanities Library, 1963.

Valuable studies in the history of the doctrine.

Masselink, William. *General Revelation and Common Grace.* Grand Rapids: Eerdmans, 1953.
Deals with the controversies on common grace, general revelation, and apologetics involving Cornelius Van Til and others in Dutch and American Reformed circles.

Morris, Leon. *I Believe in Revelation.* Grand Rapids: Eerdmans, 1976.
Good overview of the subject by a prominent evangelical scholar.

Niebuhr, H. R. *The Meaning of Revelation.* New York: Macmillan, 1941.
Wrestles with problems of revelation, faith, and historical relativism.

Pannenberg, Wolfhart, ed. *Revelation as History.* New York: Macmillan, 1968.
Essays by Pannenberg and other German scholars intended to counteract the separation of revelation and history by Barth and Bultmann.

Pink, A. W. *The Doctrine of Revelation.* Grand Rapids: Baker, 1975.
Biblical exposition by a popular conservative writer.

Ramm, Bernard. *Special Revelation and the Word of God.* Grand Rapids: Eerdmans, 1961.
The author, a leading American evangelical theologian, holds together both the redemptive and the cognitive aspects of special revelation.

Van Til, Cornelius. *Common Grace and the Gospel.* Nutley, NJ: Presbyterian and Reformed, 1973.
Essays on common grace, with reference to apologetics and natural theology.

Scripture

Conservative

Bannerman, James. *Inspiration: The Infallible Truth and Divine*

Authority of the Holy Scriptures. Edinburgh: Clark, 1865.
See pp. 114-148 on history of doctrine.

Berkouwer, G. C. *Holy Scripture.* Grand Rapids: Eerdmans, 1975.
Argues that inerrancy should be distinguished from historical and scientific exactness.

Boettner, Loraine. *The Inspiration of the Scriptures.* Grand Rapids: Eerdmans, 1937.

Cunningham, William. *Theological Lectures.* London: Nisbet, 1878.
Pp. 269-469 discuss inspiration and canonicity.

Custer, Stewart. *Does Inspiration Demand Inerrancy?* Nutley, NJ: Craig Press, 1968.
Pp. 93-114 discuss various problem texts.

Davis, Stephen T. *The Debate About the Bible.* Philadelphia: Westminster, 1977.
Reviews the contemporary debate and concludes that "infallibility in faith and practice" rather than inerrancy should be the evangelical stance.

Engelder, Theodore. *The Scripture Cannot Be Broken.* St. Louis: Concordia, 1944.

France, R. T. *Jesus and the Old Testament.* London: Tyndale, 1971.
A revised version of the author's doctoral dissertation.

Gaussen, Louis. *The Inspiration of the Holy Scriptures.* Chicago: Moody Press, n.d.
First published in 1840; still helpful.

Gerstner, John H. *A Bible Inerrancy Primer.* Grand Rapids: Baker, 1965.

Harris, R. Laird. *The Inspiration and Canonicity of the Bible.* Grand Rapids: Zondervan, 1957.
A staunch defense of verbal inspiration; argues that inspiration is the principle of canonicity.

*Henry, Carl F. H. *God, Revelation, and Authority.* Vol. 4. Waco, TX: Word, 1979.
A massive treatment of biblical authority; good discussion of inerrancy.

Henry, Carl F. H., ed. *Revelation and the Bible*. Grand Rapids: Baker, 1958.

Essays by various evangelical scholars including G. C. Berkouwer, Paul K. Jewett, Gordon H. Clark, J. I. Packer, Roger Nicole, Edward J. Young, Bernard Ramm, and F. F. Bruce. Note essay by Geoffrey Bromiley on history of doctrine of inspiration.

*Hodge, A. A., and Warfield, B. B. *Inspiration*. Grand Rapids: Baker, 1979.

Reprint of the famous article which originally appeared in the April 1881 issue of the *Presbyterian Review*; with an introduction and bibliography by Roger R. Nicole.

Kistemaker, Simon, ed. *Interpreting God's Word Today*. Grand Rapids: Baker, 1970.

Note essay by editor on formation and interpretation of the Gospels.

Kline, Meredith. *The Structure of Biblical Authority*. Grand Rapids: Eerdmans, 1970.

Argues that the concept of canon should be understood on the basis of the treaty documents of the ancient Near East.

Kretzmann, P. E. *The Foundations Must Stand*. St. Louis: Concordia, 1936.

Kuyper, Abraham. *Principles of Sacred Theology*. Grand Rapids: Eerdmans, 1954.

See especially pp. 341-563.

Lecerf, Auguste. *Introduction to Reformed Dogmatics*. London: Lutterworth, 1949.

See pp. 319-374 on canonicity and inspiration.

Lee, William. *The Inspiration of Holy Scriptures*. New York: Carter, 1857.

Pp. 51-93 review the patristic data.

Lightner, Robert P. *The Saviour and the Scriptures*. Grand Rapids: Baker, 1966.

A defense of inerrancy based on Christ's view of Scripture.

Lindsell, Harold. *The Battle For the Bible*. Grand Rapids: Zondervan, 1976.

Added fresh fuel to the debate with the claim that there is

evidence of significant erosion on inerrancy in various evangelical denominations and schools.

M'Intosh, Hugh. *Is Christ Infallible and the Bible True?* Edinburgh: Clark, 1901.
Extensive discussion of various criticisms of Christ's infallibility as a teacher. Still valuable.

Montgomery, John W., ed. *God's Inerrant Word.* Minneapolis: Bethany Fellowship, 1974.
Essays by Montgomery, J. I. Packer, John Gerstner, Clark Pinnock, R. T. France, Peter Jones, and R. C. Sproul; very helpful.

Morris, Leon. *I Believe in Revelation.* Grand Rapids: Eerdmans, 1976.
A somewhat brief treatment of various issues, including general revelation and the question of revelation outside Christianity.

Orr, James. *Revelation and Inspiration.* New York: Scribner, 1910.
Orr, a noted Scottish evangelical of an earlier generation, held that minor errors of detail are not incompatible with divine inspiration.

Pache, René. *The Inspiration and Authority of Scripture.* Chicago: Moody, 1969.
Pp. 120-158 contain good discussion of inerrancy and biblical difficulties.

*Packer, James I. *"Fundamentalism" and the Word of God.* Grand Rapids: Eerdmans, 1958.
A clear and cogent statement of the evangelical view of Scripture. Packer is in the process of preparing a new edition to respond to James Barr's *Fundamentalism.*

Pesch, Christiano. *De Inspiratione Sacrae Scripturae.* Freiburg, Germany: Herder, 1906.
A scholarly treatment of the history of the doctrine; can be used to locate patristic references even by those with no knowledge of Latin.

Pinnock, Clark H. *Biblical Revelation.* Chicago: Moody, 1971.

_____. *A Defense of Biblical Infallibility.* Philadelphia: Presbyterian and Reformed, 1967.

For a more recent expression of Pinnock's position on inerrancy, see *Theology, News and Notes*, special issue, 1976.

Preus, Robert D. *The Theology of Post-Reformation Lutheranism: A Study of Theological Prolegomena.* St. Louis: Concordia, 1970.
See pp. 254-403 for discussion on the doctrine of Scripture. A valuable historical study.

Ramm, Bernard. *The Pattern of Authority.* Grand Rapids: Eerdmans, 1957.
Brief discussion of Scripture in relation to various understandings of religious authority, including Roman Catholicism, modernism, and neoorthodoxy.

*Rogers, Jack B., and McKim, Donald K. *The Authority and Interpretation of the Bible: An Historical Approach.* San Francisco: Harper and Row, 1979.
The most important recent expression of the "limited inerrancy" position in American evangelicalism.

Runia, Klaas. *Karl Barth's Doctrine of Holy Scripture.* Grand Rapids: Eerdmans, 1962.
A careful criticism of Barth's view of Scripture from a Reformed perspective.

Scroggie. W. G. *Is the Bible the Word of God?* Philadelphia: Sunday School Times, 1922.

Stonehouse, N. B., and Woolley, Paul, eds. *The Infallible Word.* Grand Rapids: Eerdmans, 1946, 1953.
A symposium by members of the faculty of Westminster Theological Seminary.

Tenney, Merrill C., ed. *The Bible: The Living Word of Revelation.* Grand Rapids: Zondervan, 1968.
Essays by evangelical scholars.

Van Kooten, Tenis. *The Bible: God's Word.* Grand Rapids: Baker, 1972.
Pp. 200-220 criticize various deviant views.

Walvoord, John F., ed. *Inspiration and Interpretation.* Grand Rapids: Eerdmans, 1957.
Essays by various members of the Evangelical Theological

Society. Note essay by Kenneth Kantzer on Calvin's view of Scripture.

*Warfield, B. B. *The Inspiration and Authority of the Bible.* Philadelphia: Presbyterian and Reformed, 1948.

Reprints of exegetical and theological articles by Warfield which have never, in some respects, been surpassed. Note especially the article " 'It Says:' 'Scripture Says:' 'God Says.' "

Warfield, B. B. *Limited Inspiration.* Philadelphia: Presbyterian and Reformed, 1962.

Reprint of an article which originally appeared in volume 5 (1894) of the *Presbyterian and Reformed Review.* In his reply to Professor Henry P. Smith, Warfield criticizes the view that inspiration may be limited to matters of "faith and morals."

*Wenham, John W. *Christ and the Bible.* London: Tyndale, 1972.

A valuable work which interacts with recent biblical scholarship.

Young, E. J. *Thy Word Is Truth.* Grand Rapids: Eerdmans, 1957.

Young was professor of Old Testament at Westminster Theological Seminary. Chapter 7 discusses several problem texts.

Nonconservative

Barr, James. *The Bible in the Modern World.* New York: Harper, 1973.

_____. *Fundamentalism.* London: SCM, 1977.

The latter volume is a full-scale attack on the evangelical view of Scripture and conservative theology in general.

Beegle, Dewey M. *Scripture, Tradition, and Infallibility.* Grand Rapids: Eerdmans, 1973.

A review and enlargement of the earlier 1963 work, *The Inspiration of Scripture.* Beegle contends that infallibility and inerrancy apply only to God and Christ, not the Bible.

Briggs, Charles A. *The Bible, the Church and the Reason.* New York: Scribner, 1892.

Briggs's views on inerrancy and higher criticism led to his trial for heresy in the Presbyterian church.

Burtchaell, James T. *Catholic Theories of Biblical Inspiration Since 1810.* Cambridge: Cambridge University Press, 1969.
In this historical study the author criticizes Catholic theories of verbal inspiration and inerrancy.

Dillistone, F. W., ed. *Scripture and Tradition.* London: Lutterworth, 1955.
Essays by various British scholars.

Dodd, C. H. *The Authority of the Bible.* New York: Harper, 1929.
Liberal Protestant. The Bible is authoritative because it "is the instrument of the Spirit in creating an experience of divine things . . . in inducing in us a religious attitude and outlook."

Dods, Marcus. *The Bible: Its Origin and Nature.* Edinburgh: Clark, 1905.
Liberal Protestant; criticizes concepts of verbal inspiration and infallibility.

Fosdick, Harry E. *The Modern Use of the Bible.* New York: Macmillan, 1924.
Fosdick, pastor of Riverside Church in New York City, was a modernist leader in the modernist-fundamentalist controversy.

Gore, Charles, and Mackintosh, H. R. *The Doctrine of the Infallible Book.* London: Student Christian Movement, 1924.
Argues that the Bible, while inspired in varying degrees and modes, is not infallible.

Huxtable, J. F. *The Bible Says.* London: SCM, 1962.
Pp. 64-71 criticize J. I. Packer and other conservative writers.

Ladd, George T. *The Doctrine of Sacred Scripture.* 2 vols. New York: Scribner, 1883.
A lengthy discussion by a liberal Protestant scholar who taught at Yale during the last century.

Levie, Jean. *The Bible: Word of God in Words of Men.* New York: P. J. Kenedy and Sons, 1961.
Liberal Roman Catholic.

Rahner, Karl. *The Inspiration of the Bible.* New York: Herder and Herder, 1961.
Nontraditional Roman Catholic.

Reid, J. K. S. *The Authority of the Scriptures.* New York: Harper, 1957.

Neoorthodox in orientation; argues that Luther and Calvin did not hold to strict verbal inspiration.

Richardson, Alan, and Schweitzer, Wolfgang, eds. *Biblical Authority for Today.* Philadelphia: Westminster, 1951.
A World Council of Churches symposium.

Sanday, William. *Inspiration.* London: Longmans and Green, 1893.

Smart, J. D. *The Interpretation of Scripture.* Philadelphia: Westminster, 1961.
Neoorthodox.

Smith, Henry P., and Evans, Llewelyn J. *Biblical Scholarship and Inspiration.* Cincinnati: Clarke, 1891.
Smith, who held that there are "minor errors" in Scripture, became embroiled in a controversy over inerrancy in the Presbyterian church in the 1890s.

Vawter, Bruce. *Biblical Inspiration.* Philadelphia: Westminster, 1972.
Roman Catholic; post-Vatican II in attitude toward biblical criticism.

Hermeneutics

Achtemeier, Paul J. *An Introduction to the New Hermeneutic.* Philadelphia: Westminster, 1969.
A readable introduction to a somewhat obscure movement.

Berkhof, Louis. *Principles of Biblical Interpretation.* Grand Rapids: Baker, 1950.
Dutch Reformed.

Briggs, R. C. *Interpreting the New Testament Today.* Nashville: Abingdon, 1969.
A helpful introduction to issues in New Testament interpretation.

Fairbairn, Patrick. *The Typology of Scripture.* Edinburgh: Clark, 1870.
A classic on the subject by a nineteenth-century Scottish scholar.

Farrar, Frederic W. *History of Interpretation*. London: Macmillan, 1885.
A standard treatment.

Grant, Robert M. *A Short History of the Interpretation of the Bible*. New York: Macmillan, 1948.
A concise and helpful account.

Kuitert, H. M. *Do You Understand What You Read?* Grand Rapids: Eerdmans, 1970.
Emphasizes time-bound character of biblical truth; favors nonliteral view of early Genesis.

Marlé, René. *Introduction to Hermeneutics*. New York: Herder and Herder, 1967.
Discusses issues in modern theological hermeneutics; Roman Catholic.

Marshall, I. H., ed. *New Testament Interpretation*. Grand Rapids: Eerdmans, 1977.
Valuable essays by various evangelical scholars, mostly British.

*Mickelsen, A. Berkeley. *Interpreting the Bible*. Grand Rapids: Eerdmans, 1963.
One of the best evangelical treatments of biblical hermeneutics.

*Palmer, Richard. *Hermeneutics*. Evanston, IL: Northwestern University Press, 1969.
A valuable guide to the hermeneutical discussions of Friedrich Schleiermacher, Wilhelm Dilthey, Martin Heidegger, and Hans-Georg Gadamer.

Ramm, Bernard. *Protestant Biblical Interpretation*. Boston: W. A. Wilde, 1956.
Chapter 8 discusses inerrancy and secular science in relation to hermeneutics. A standard conservative text.

Robinson, James M., and Cobb, John B., Jr., eds. *The New Hermeneutic*. New York: Harper and Row, 1964.
Essays by Robinson, Gerhard Ebeling, Ernst Fuchs, and others.

Schultz, Samuel J., and Inch, Morris A., eds. *Interpreting the Word of God*. Chicago: Moody, 1976.

Note essay by Gordon Fee on pp. 103-127.

God

Adeney, W. F. *The Christian Concept of God*. London: National Council of Evangelical Free Churches, 1909.

*Aquinas, Thomas. *Summa Theologica* Ia. 1-49. New York: McGraw-Hill, 1963-
Discussions on the doctrine of God by one of the greatest theologians of all time.

Baillie, John. *Our Knowledge of God*. New York: Scribner, 1939.
Lectures by a well-known Scottish contemporary of Karl Barth and Emil Brunner.

Bavinck, Herman. *The Doctrine of God*. Grand Rapids: Baker, 1951.
A comprehensive treatment taken from volume 2 of the author's systematic theology. Dutch Reformed.

*Calvin, John. *Institutes of the Christian Religion*. Books 1 and 2. Translated by Ford Lewis Battles. Philadelphia: Westminster, 1960.
Classic discussion of the knowledge of God.

*Charnock, Stephen. The Existence and Attributes of God. Evansville, IN: Sovereign Grace, 1958.
A classic by a Puritan writer of the seventeenth century.

Dewan, W. F. *The One God*. Englewood Cliffs, NJ: Prentice-Hall, 1963.
Roman Catholic.

Dowey, E. A. *The Knowledge of God in Calvin's Theology*. New York: Columbia University Press, 1952.
A valuable study of Calvin's theological epistemology.

Farley, Edward. *The Transcendence of God*. Philadelphia: Westminster, 1960.
A study of the transcendence of God as viewed by Reinhold

Niebuhr, Paul Tillich, Karl Heim, Charles Hartshorne, and Henry Nelson Wieman.

Ferré, Nels. *The Christian Understanding of God*. New York: Harper, 1951.
Philosophically oriented.

Fortman, E. J., ed. *The Theology of God: Commentary*. Milwaukee: Bruce, 1968.

France, R. T. *The Living God*. Downers Grove, IL: Inter-Varsity, 1970.
A brief, popular but helpful survey of biblical teaching. Good for church study classes.

Garrigou-Lagrange, Reginald. *God: His Existence and His Nature*. 2 vols. St. Louis: Herder, 1936.
An important apologetic work by a modern Catholic theologian in the Thomistic tradition.

Gollwitzer, Helmut. *The Existence of God as Confessed by Faith*. Philadelphia: Westminster, 1965.
Interacts with Rudolf Bultmann, Paul Tillich, and other European theologians; Barthian in perspective.

Headlam, Arthur C. *Christian Theology: The Doctrine of God*. Oxford: Clarendon Press, 1934.
A text prepared for divinity students in the Church of England.

Henry, Carl F. H. *Notes on the Doctrine of God*. Boston: W. A. Wilde, 1948.
Essays by a well-known evangelical apologist.

Hick, John. *Arguments for the Existence of God*. New York: Seabury, 1971.
Pp. 136-146 contain a helpful bibliography on the theistic proofs.

*John of Damascus. *The Orthodox Faith*. In *St. John of Damascus: Writings*. Translated by F. H. Chase, Jr. New York: Fathers of the Church, 1958.
The fountainhead of Eastern Orthodox theology.

Kaufman, Gordon D. *God the Problem*. Cambridge: MA: Harvard University Press, 1972.

Various essays in philosophical theology by a professor at Harvard Divinity School.

*Knudson, A. C. *The Doctrine of God*. New York: Abingdon-Cokesbury, 1934.

Knudson taught for many years at Boston University School of Theology; moderately liberal.

Lightner, Robert P. *The First Fundamental: God*. Nashville: Thomas Nelson, 1973.

A biblical study by a professor at Dallas Theological Seminary.

Mackintosh, H. R. *The Christian Apprehension of God*. New York: Harper, 1929.

Lectures given at Union Theological Seminary of Virginia in 1928.

Matczak, Sebastian A., ed. *God in Contemporary Thought: A Philosophical Perspective*. New York: Learned Publications, 1977.

Scholarly essays on concepts of God in both Christian and non-Christian traditions, with bibliographies.

Mozley, J. K. *The Impassibility of God*. Cambridge: Cambridge University Press, 1926.

A valuable historical study of one particular aspect of the divine nature.

Ogden, Schubert. *The Reality of God and Other Essays*. New York: Harper, 1966.

Essays by a contemporary American process-theologian.

*Otto, Rudolf. *The Idea of the Holy*. London: Oxford University Press, 1923.

A famous study of an essential characteristic of the religious experience.

*Owen, H. P. *Concepts of Deity*. New York: Herder and Herder, 1971.

An excellent comparative study of classical theism and various modern views.

Packer, J. I. *Knowing God*. Downers Grove, IL: Inter-Varsity, 1973.

A fine demonstration of the essential relation of Christian theology and the Christian life.

Pike, Nelson. *God and Timelessness.* New York: Schocken Books, 1970.
Argues that the concept of God's timelessness was imported from Platonism.

Robinson, J. A. T. *Explorations into God.* London: SCM, 1966.
A dubious attempt to move "beyond the God of theism."

Tozer, A. W. *The Knowledge of the Holy.* New York: Harper, 1961.
A popular but valuable discussion of the attributes of God in relation to the Christian life.

Wenham, John. *The Goodness of God.* Downers Grove, IL: Inter-Varsity, 1974.
A fine biblical study of God's goodness in relation to the problems of suffering, evil, and retribution.

Trinity

Augustine. *On the Holy Trinity.* In *The Nicene and Post-Nicene Fathers,* vol. 3. Grand Rapids: Eerdmans, 1956.
A classic source.

Barth, Karl. *Church Dogmatics,* I/1. Edinburgh: Clark, 1936.
Chapter 2 presents Barth's discussion of the Trinity.

*Fortman, E. J. *The Triune God.* Philadelphia: Westminster, 1972.
A comprehensive discussion of the history of the doctrine.

Franks, R. S. *The Doctrine of the Trinity.* London: Duckworth, 1953.
Argues for a view combining elements of Friedrich Schleiermacher, Aquinas, and Karl Barth.

Hodgson, Leonard. *The Doctrine of the Trinity.* New York: Scribner, 1944.
Argues for the "social" rather than the "psychological" analogy.

Knight, G. A. F. *A Biblical Approach to the Doctrine of the Trinity.* Edinburgh: Oliver and Boyd, 1953.
Stresses value of Old Testament theology.

Mikolaski, S. J. "The Triune God," in *Fundamentals of the Faith,* edited by Carl F. H. Henry. Grand Rapids: Zondervan, 1969.
A brief overview.

Rahner, Karl. *The Trinity.* New York: Herder and Herder, 1970.
Stresses relation of Trinity to Christology and pneumatology; argues for "three distinct manners of subsisting" rather than "three persons."

Richardson, C. C. *The Doctrine of the Trinity.* New York: Abingdon, 1958.
Questions traditional formulations of trinitarian doctrine.

Wainwright, A. W. *The Trinity in the New Testament.* London: SPCK, 1962.
A helpful biblical study.

Warfield, B. B. "Trinity," in *Biblical and Theological Studies.* Philadelphia: Presbyterian and Reformed, 1952.
A good discussion of the biblical data.

Welch, Claude. *In This Name: The Doctrine of the Trinity in Contemporary Theology.* New York: Scribner, 1952.
A significant contribution by an American scholar; favors the "psychological" rather than the "social" model of the Trinity.

Election and Predestination

Aquinas, Thomas. *Summa Theologica,* 1.23; 3.24. New York: McGraw-Hill, 1963-

Augustine. *Anti-Pelagian Works.* In *The Nicene and Post-Nicene Fathers,* vol. 5. New York: Christian Literature Company, 1887.
"On the Predestination of the Saints."

Barth, Karl. *Church Dogmatics,* II/2. Edinburgh: Clark, 1957.
See chapter 7 for Barth's discussion of election.

Berkouwer, G. C. *Divine Election.* Grand Rapids: Eerdmans, 1960.
Contends that election can be understood only within the context of faith and the gospel; rejects logical symmetry of election and reprobation.

Boettner, Loraine. *The Reformed Doctrine of Predestination.* Philadelphia: Presbyterian and Reformed, 1932.
A clear statement of the Calvinistic position.

*Calvin, John. *Institutes of the Christian Religion,* Book 3, 21-24. Philadelphia: Westminster, 1960.
A classic treatment.

Edwards, Jonathan. *Freedom of the Will.* London: James Duncan, 1831.
Penetrating discussions by one of America's greatest theologians.

Forster, Roger T., and Marston, V. Paul. *God's Strategy in Human History.* Bromley, England: Send the Light Trust, 1973.
Exegetical discussion from an Arminian perspective.

Pinnock, Clark, ed. *Grace Unlimited.* Minneapolis: Bethany Fellowship, 1975.
Various essays from an Arminian perspective.

Creation and Providence

*Barbour, Ian G. *Issues in Science and Religion.* Englewood Cliffs, NJ: Prentice-Hall, 1966.
An important work in the area of science and religion; written from a perspective sympathetic to process theology.

Barnette, H. *The Church and the Ecological Crisis.* Grand Rapids: Eerdmans, 1972.
Brief discussion of biblical basis for environmental concern.

Berkouwer, G. C. *The Providence of God.* Grand Rapids: Eerdmans, 1952.
A good treatment of the subject, including discussion of issues raised by the scientific world-view. Reformed in perspective.

Clark, R. E. D. *The Universe: Plan or Accident.* Philadelphia: Muhlenberg Press, 1962.
Discussions of issues in science and Scripture, including a defense of the argument from design.

Dillenberger, John. *Protestant Thought and Natural Science.* London: Collins, 1961.

A useful work tracing developments from the Reformation to the present; written from a neoorthodox perspective.

Farmer, H. H. *The World and God.* London: Nisbet, 1936.

A study of prayer, providence, and miracle; stresses religious experience rather than Scripture as starting point for theology.

Gilkey, Langdon. *Maker of Heaven and Earth.* Garden City, NY: Doubleday, 1965.

An important recent discussion relating creation to issues in philosophy, the sciences, and studies in myth and symbol. Neo-orthodox in orientation.

*Hick, John. *Evil and the God of Love.* London: Macmillan, 1966.

One of the best discussions of the problem of evil in historical and theological perspective.

Hooykaas, R. *Religion and the Rise of Modern Science.* Edinburgh: Scottish Academic Press, 1972.

Shows that biblical thought was as important as, if not more important than, Greek thought in the rise of modern science.

Kerkut, G. A. *The Implications of Evolution.* London: Pergamon, 1960.

A highly technical but quite valuable discussion of the assumptions behind modern evolutionary theories.

Klotz, John W. *Genes, Genesis, and Evolution.* St. Louis: Concordia, 1955, 1970.

Klotz, a Missouri Synod Lutheran and trained biologist, favors special creation and an old earth. Good survey of scientific data.

Kuyper, Abraham. *Lectures on Calvinism.* Grand Rapids: Eerdmans, 1931.

The Stone lectures given at Princeton in 1898; valuable discussions of Christianity and culture from a Reformed perspective.

*Lewis, C. S. *Miracles.* New York: Macmillan, 1947.

A fine defense of miracle by a noted evangelical apologist.

*Macbeth, Norman. *Darwin Retried.* Boston: Gambit, 1971.

An incisive and readable critique of Darwinian and neo-Darwinian theories.

Mascall, E. L. *Christian Theology and Natural Science*. London: Longmans, 1956.
Various issues at the interface of science and theology discussed by an Anglican scholar indebted to the Thomistic tradition.

Meynell, Hugo. *God and the World*. London: SPCK, 1971.
A fine defense of classical theism against contemporary attacks by a Roman Catholic scholar. Includes chapters on evil, miracles, prayer.

Orr, James. *The Christian View of God and the World*. New York: Scribner, 1893.
A classic by a Scottish evangelical of an earlier generation.

Pollard, W. G. *Chance and Providence*. New York: Scribner, 1958.
The author is a physicist and an Episcopal priest. A somewhat dualistic approach to relating science and religion.

Ramm, Bernard. *A Christian View of Science and Scripture*. Grand Rapids: Eerdmans, 1954.
Evangelical discussion of questions relating to astronomy, geology, biology, and anthropology. Old-earth, "progressive"-creationist perspective.

Ridderbos, N. *Is There a Conflict Between Genesis I and Natural Science?* Grand Rapids: Eerdmans, 1957.
Argues for a nonliteral-framework hypothesis for Genesis 1. Brief but helpful.

Rushdoony, R. J. *The Mythology of Science*. Nutley, NJ: Craig, 1967.
Critique of scientism by a conservative Calvinist. Several chapters devoted to creation and evolution.

White, Andrew Dickson. *A History of the Warfare of Science with Theology*. First published in 1896. New York: Dover.

Wilder-Smith, A. E. *Man's Origin, Man's Destiny*. Wheaton, IL: Harold Shaw, 1968.
A good criticism of evolutionary theories of human origins by

a competent scientist. Second half of the volume is more speculative.

Man

Berkouwer, G. C. *Man: The Image of God.* Grand Rapids: Eerdmans, 1962.
Competent discussion by a well-known Dutch Reformed theologian.

Brunner, Emil. *Man in Revolt.* Philadelphia: Westminster, 1947.
Important discussions by a leading neoorthodox theologian.

Cairns, David. *The Image of God in Man.* London: Collins, 1973.
Good survey of the history of the doctrine.

Johnson. A. R. *The Vitality of the Individual in the Thought of Ancient Israel.* Cardiff: University of Wales, 1949.
Detailed exegetical study of Hebrew anthropology. Valuable.

Kümmel, Werner G. *Man in the New Testament.* Philadelphia: Westminster, 1963.
A study in New Testament theology; Kümmel sees both unity and diversity in the New Testament view of man.

Machen, J. Gresham. *The Christian View of Man.* Grand Rapids: Eerdmans, 1947.
Popular discussions originally presented as radio lectures by a well-known Reformed scholar.

Moltmann, Jürgen. *Man: Christian Anthropology in the Conflicts of the Present.* Philadelphia: Fortress, 1974.
Moltmann relates his theological understanding to issues in social ethics.

*Niebuhr, Reinhold. *The Nature and Destiny of Man.* 2 vols. New York: Scribner, 1949.
A classic of modern American theology; note especially discussion of sin. Neoorthodox.

Orr, James. *God's Image in Man.* London: Hodder and Stoughton, 1905.

Apologetic discussions by a well-known Scottish theologian; somewhat dated.

Pannenberg, Wolfhart. *What Is Man?* Philadelphia: Fortress, 1970.
The author interacts with various trends in modern thought; philosophical rather than exegetical in approach.

*Robinson, H. W. *The Christian Doctrine of Man.* 3rd ed. Edinburgh: Clark, 1934.
An important work combining exegetical, historical, and theological data. Emphasizes Hebrew psychology as basis of New Testament and patristic thought.

Rust, Eric C. *Nature and Man in Biblical Thought.* London: Lutterworth, 1953.
A biblical theology of man related to the philosophy of nature.

*Smith, C. Ryder. *The Bible Doctrine of Man.* London: Epworth, 1951.
A comprehensive biblical study.

Torrance, T. F. *Calvin's Doctrine of Man.* London: Lutterworth, 1949.
A valuable historical study. Note especially discussion of noetic effects of sin and natural theology.

Sin

Berkouwer, G. C. *Sin.* Grand Rapids, Eerdmans, 1971.
One of the best recent treatments of the subject; Reformed perspective.

Buswell, J. Oliver. *Sin and Atonement.* Grand Rapids: Zondervan, 1937.
A brief biblical study.

*Fairlie, Henry. *The Seven Deadly Sins Today.* Notre Dame, IN: University of Notre Dame, 1978.
Insightful reflections by an author who does not consider himself a believer.

Kierkegaard, Sören. *Sickness unto Death.* Princeton: Princeton University Press, 1946.

Classic discussion of despair by the famous Danish existentialist.

Menninger, Karl. *Whatever Became of Sin?* New York: Hawthorn Books, 1973.
Stimulating insights by a leading American psychiatrist.

Müller, Julius. *The Christian Doctrine of Sin.* 2 vols. Edinburgh: Clark, 1885.
A significant work from the nineteenth century.

*Murray, John. *The Imputation of Adam's Sin.* Grand Rapids: Eerdmans, 1959.
Careful exegetical discussions of theories of imputation of original sin; defends representative view.

Orr, James. *Sin as a Problem Today.* London: Hodder and Stoughton, 1910.
Somewhat dated.

Smith, C. Ryder. *The Bible Doctrine of Sin.* London: Epworth, 1953.
A helpful biblical study; a bit weak on original sin.

Tennant, F. C. *The Sources of the Doctrine of the Fall and Original Sin.* Cambridge: Cambridge University Press, 1903.
An important scholarly work; critical and nonliteral view of Genesis account of the fall. Note also *The Concept of Sin* and *The Origin and Propagation of Sin* by the same author.

Warfield, B. B. *Studies in Tertullian and Augustine.* New York: Oxford University Press, 1930.
Contains a valuable essay on Augustine and the Pelagian controversy.

Williams, N. P. *The Ideas of the Fall and Original Sin.* London: Longmans, 1927.
A comprehensive scholarly work; critical view of biblical accounts. Proposes theory of precosmic fall.

Person of Christ

*Baillie, Donald M. *God Was in Christ.* New York: Scribner, 1948.

An important attempt to relate traditional Christologies to questions arising in modern biblical scholarship. Generally conservative conclusions.

Berkouwer, G. C. *The Person of Christ*. Grand Rapids: Eerdmans, 1954.
Helpful discussions by a Dutch Reformed theologian.

Cullmann, Oscar. *The Christology of the New Testament*. Philadelphia: Westminster, 1959.
A study of New Testament Christological titles from the perspective of *Heilsgeschichte* (salvation history).

Dawe, Donald G. *The Form of a Servant*. Philadelphia: Westminster, 1963.
Reviews history of kenotic Christologies. Advocates a functional rather than metaphysical approach.

Dorner, I. A. *History of the Development of the Doctrine of the Person of Christ*. 5 vols. Edinburgh: Clark, 1876-1882.
Comprehensive survey of history of doctrine from early church to nineteenth century. Generally conservative.

Forsyth, P. T. *The Person and Place of Jesus Christ*. Grand Rapids: Eerdmans, 1964.
Originally published in 1909. Forsyth, sometimes called a "Barthian before Barth," stresses the moral power of the cross. Stimulating.

Grillmeier, H. *Christ in Christian Tradition*. New York: Sheed and Ward, 1964.
A masterful study by a Jesuit scholar of the development of Christology from the apostolic age to Chalcedon.

*Liddon, H. P. *The Divinity of Our Lord and Savior Jesus Christ*. New York: Longmans and Green, 1890.
Classic defense of the deity of Christ by a conservative Anglican of the last century.

Longenecker, R. N. *Christology of Early Jewish Christianity*. Naperville, IL: Alec R. Allenson, 1970.
A fine study by an American evangelical biblical scholar.

Machen, J. G. *The Virgin Birth of Christ*. New York: Harper, 1930.
A scholarly defense of the virgin birth.

Marshall, I. H. *I Believe in the Historical Jesus*. Grand Rapids: Eerdmans, 1977.

Careful review of research into the life of Jesus from an evangelical perspective.

Pannenberg, Wolfhart. *Jesus—God and Man*. Philadelphia: Westminster, 1968, 1977.

An important work by a prominent German theologian. Advocates a Christology "from below"; stresses resurrection as key to Jesus' divinity.

Torrance, Thomas F. *Space, Time, and Incarnation*. London: Oxford University Press, 1969.

Penetrating discussions of the incarnation in relation to issues in science by a conservative Barthian.

*Turner, H. E. W. *Jesus, Master and Lord*. London: Mowbray, 1964.

A helpful survey and synthesis of modern New Testament studies by a conservative Anglican.

Vos, Geerhardus. *The Self-Disclosure of Jesus*. New York: Doran, 1926.

A study of the messianic self-consciousness of Jesus by a conservative Calvinist.

Warfield, B. B. *The Lord of Glory*. New York: American Tract Society, 1907.

Helpful discussions by a conservative Calvinist. See also Warfield's *Christology and Criticism*.

Work of Christ

Anselm. *Cur Deus Homo?* La Salle, IL: Open Court, 1962.

A classic exposition of the satisfaction theory of the atonement from the eleventh century.

Aulén, Gustaf. *Christus Victor*. London: SPCK, 1950.

Argues for the importance of the "classic" theory of the atonement in the early church and Luther.

Berkouwer, G. C. *The Work of Christ*. Grand Rapids: Eerdmans, 1965.

Competent treatment by a Dutch Reformed scholar. Ninth in the series of Berkouwer's *Studies in Dogmatics*.

Brunner, Emil. *The Mediator*. Philadelphia: Westminster, 1947.
Considered by many to be a twentieth-century classic in Christology. Neoorthodox.

Cave, Alfred. *The Scriptural Doctrine of Sacrifice and Atonement*. Edinburgh: Clark, 1890.
An older conservative work.

Dale, R. W. *The Atonement*. London: Congregational Union, 1905.
Lectures delivered in 1875 by a prominent British evangelical.

Denney, James. *The Death of Christ*. New York: Hodder and Stoughton, 1911.
A careful study of the death of Christ in the New Testament; evangelical.

Forsyth, P. T. *The Work of Christ*. London: Independent Press, 1938.
Forsyth stressed the moral impact of the cross.

Franks, R. S. *The Work of Christ: A Historical Study of Christian Doctrine*. New York: Nelson, 1962.
A comprehensive survey of the history of doctrine.

*Hodge, A. A. *The Atonement*. First published in 1867. Grand Rapids: Guardian Press, n.d.
A classic work on a pivotal doctrine by a staunch Calvinist.

Hughes, Thomas H. *The Atonement: Modern Theories of the Doctrine*. London: Allen and Unwin, 1949.
A study of modern British theories of the atonement. Concludes with the author's own speculative view.

Mackintosh, Robert. *Historic Theories of the Atonement*. London: Hodder and Stoughton, 1920.
A review of the history of the doctrine. The author's position has affinities with satisfaction theories.

Morris, Leon. *The Cross in the New Testament*. Grand Rapids: Eerdmans, 1965.
Fine biblical study by a well-known evangelical scholar. See also the author's *Apostolic Preaching of the Cross*.

Murray, John. *Redemption Accomplished and Applied.* Grand Rapids: Eerdmans, 1955.
A fine study by a well-known Reformed scholar.

*Nicole, Roger. "The Nature of Redemption," in Carl F. H. Henry, ed., *Christian Faith and Modern Theology.* New York: Channel Press, 1964.
A fine treatment of the New Testament language of redemption by a conservative Reformed scholar.

Rashdall, Hastings. *The Idea of the Atonement in Christian Theology.* London: Macmillan, 1925.
A major modern statement of the moral-influence theory. Excludes elements of penal substitution.

Smeaton, George. *The Doctrine of the Atonement.* Edinburgh: Clark, 1870.
An older but still valuable conservative work.

Taylor, Vincent. *The Atonement in New Testament Teaching.* London: Epworth, 1940.
Part of an important scholarly trilogy including *Jesus and His Sacrifice* (1937) and *Forgiveness and Reconciliation* (1941). Taylor opposes concepts of propitiation and penal substitution.

Warfield, B. B. *The Person and Work of Christ.* Philadelphia: Presbyterian and Reformed, 1950.
Posthumously published essays by a notable Reformed theologian.

Salvation and the Holy Spirit

Berkouwer, G. C. *Faith and Justification.* Grand Rapids: Eerdmans, 1954.
A careful treatment by a Dutch Reformed theologian. See also *Faith and Perseverance* (1958) and *Faith and Sanctification* (1966) by the same author.

*Bruner, F. D. *A Theology of the Holy Spirit.* Grand Rapids: Eerdmans, 1970.
An important scholarly study of the Pentecostal experience.

*Buchanan, James. *The Doctrine of Justification*. First published in 1867. Grand Rapids: Baker, 1977.
Still one of the finest treatments of the subject.

Burkhardt, Helmut. *The Biblical Doctrine of Regeneration*. Downers Grove, IL: Inter-Varsity, 1978.
A brief but helpful study of the doctrine of regeneration.

Citron, B. *The New Birth*. Edinburgh: Edinburgh University Press, 1951.
A scholarly study of Calvinistic, Lutheran, Roman Catholic, and Methodist understandings of conversion.

Dunn, J. D. G. *Baptism in the Holy Spirit*. Naperville, IL: Alec R. Allenson, 1970.
Together with the work of F. D. Bruner, one of the most significant recent contributions to the subject.

Green, Michael. *I Believe in the Holy Spirit*. Grand Rapids: Eerdmans, 1975.
Contains a helpful bibliography.

Kuyper, Abraham. *The Work of the Holy Spirit*. First published in 1900. Grand Rapids: Eerdmans, 1941.
An extensive treatment by a Dutch Calvinist.

Marshall, I. H. *Kept by the Power of God: A Study of Perseverance and Falling Away*. London: Epworth, 1969.
Concludes that the possibility of falling away is a real one.

Packer, James I. *Evangelism and the Sovereignty of God*. Grand Rapids: Eerdmans, 1961.
Argues that the sovereignty of God provides a firm foundation for evangelism.

Ryle, J. C. *Holiness*. London: James Clarke, 1952.
Reprint of the classic work of an evangelical and Reformed bishop of the Church of England.

Shank, Robert L. *Life in the Son: A Study of the Doctrine of Perseverance*. Springfield, MO: Westcott Publishers, 1960.
Arminian perspective. See also *Elect in the Son* (1970) by the same author.

Smeaton, George. *The Doctrine of the Holy Spirit*. First published in 1882. Edinburgh: Banner of Truth, 1958.

An older conservative work by a minister of the Church of Scotland.

Stott, J. R. W. *The Baptism and Fullness of the Holy Spirit.* Downers Grove, IL: Inter-Varsity, 1964.
A concise, lucid treatment.

Swete, H. B. *The Holy Spirit in the New Testament.* London: Macmillan, 1910.
An older but still valuable biblical study. See also the author's *The Holy Spirit in the Ancient Church* (1912).

*Thomas, W. H. Griffith. *The Holy Spirit of God.* First published in 1913. Grand Rapids: Eerdmans, 1963.
A fine treatment of the biblical, historical, and theological data by a conservative Anglican.

Wallace, R. S. *Calvin's Doctrine of the Christian Life.* Grand Rapids: Eerdmans, 1959.
A careful and sympathetic study of Calvin's views. Draws from sermons and commentaries as well as the *Institutes.*

Warfield, B. B. *The Plan of Salvation.* Grand Rapids: Eerdmans, 1942.
Lectures originally delivered in 1914; Reformed perspective.

Webb, R. A. *The Theology of Infant Salvation.* Richmond: Presbyterian Committee of Publication, 1907.
Argues that all infants dying in infancy are elect. Southern Presbyterian.

*Wells, David F. *The Search for Salvation.* Downers Grove, IL: Inter-Varsity, 1978.
A fine comparison of evangelical and nonevangelical views of salvation. Very helpful.

Wesley, John. *A Plain Account of Christian Perfection.* London: Epworth, 1952.
A classic work in the Wesleyan tradition.

Church

Bannerman, Douglas. *The Scripture Doctrine of the Church.* First published in 1887. Grand Rapids: Baker, 1976.

Reprint of a Scottish Presbyterian work.

Bannerman, James. *The Church of Christ*. First published in 1860. Carlisle, PA: Banner of Truth Trust, 1960.
Scottish Presbyterian. Still valuable; note discussion of infant baptism.

Berkouwer, G. C. *The Church*. Grand Rapids: Eerdmans, 1976.
A significant study of the unity, catholicity, apostolicity, and holiness of the church. Dutch Reformed.

Best, Ernest. *One Body in Christ*. London: SPCK, 1955.
A study of Pauline ecclesiology. Concludes that the church as the "body of Christ" is neither a collection of individuals nor an extension of the incarnation.

Bloesch, Donald. *The Reform of the Church*. Grand Rapids: Eerdmans, 1970.
A call for renewal in Protestant worship, sacramental theology, and discipline. Evangelical and Reformed.

Brunner, Emil. *The Misunderstanding of the Church*. Philadelphia: Westminster, 1953.
Stresses the nature of the church as fellowship rather than organization.

Cerfaux, L. *The Church in the Theology of St. Paul*. New York: Herder and Herder, 1959.
An important study which sees considerable development in the apostle's thought on the subject.

Cole, R. A. *The Body of Christ*. Philadelphia: Westminster, 1964.
A brief study by an Anglican of the biblical metaphor of the church as the body of Christ.

Küng, Hans. *The Church*. New York: Sheed and Ward, 1967.
A significant study by a revisionist Roman Catholic theologian.

*Minear, Paul. *Images of the Church in the New Testament*. Philadelphia: Westminster, 1960.
One of the most helpful biblical studies in this area.

Schnackenburg, Rudolf. *The Church in the New Testament*. New York: Herder and Herder, 1965.

A significant work by a European New Testament scholar.

*Snyder, Howard. *The Problem of Wineskins*. Downers Grove, IL: Inter-Varsity, 1975.
Challenging and insightful discussions of church structure and church renewal. See also *The Community of the King* by the same author.

Stibbs, A. M. *God's Church: A Study in the Biblical Doctrine of the People of God*. London: Inter-Varsity, 1959.
A brief biblical study by a British evangelical.

Sacraments

Aland, Kurt. *Did the Early Church Baptize Infants?* Philadelphia: Westminster, 1963.
This German New Testament scholar answers no to the question posed in the title.

Baillie, D. *The Theology of the Sacraments*. New York: Scribner, 1957.
Posthumously published lectures of a well-known Scottish Presbyterian theologian.

Beasley-Murray, G. R. *Baptism in the New Testament*. Grand Rapids: Eerdmans, 1973.
An extensive exegetical study; holds believers' baptism.

Berkouwer, G. C. *The Sacraments*. Grand Rapids: Eerdmans, 1969.
Competent discussions by a Dutch Reformed theologian.

*Calvin, John. *Institutes of the Christian Religion*, Book 4, 14-17. Philadelphia: Westminster, 1960.
Classic presentation of the Reformed view.

Clements, R. E., et al. *Eucharistic Theology Then and Now*. London: SPCK, 1968.
A series of essays surveying the history of eucharistic theology.

Cochrane, A. C. *Eating and Drinking with Jesus*. Philadelphia: Westminster, 1974.

Discussions of the Lord's Supper by a student of Karl Barth.

Cullmann, Oscar. *Essays on the Lord's Supper*. Richmond: John Knox Press, 1958.

Fey, H. E. *The Lord's Supper: Seven Meanings*. New York: Harper, 1948.
A brief overview of various meanings.

Jeremias, J. *Infant Baptism in the First Four Centuries*. London: SCM, 1960.
Defends infant baptism. See also the author's *Origins of Infant Baptism* (1963).

Jewett, Paul. *Infant Baptism and the Covenant of Grace*. Grand Rapids: Eerdmans, 1978.
A criticism of infant baptism.

Kingdon, David. *Children of Abraham*. Cambridge: Carey, 1973.
"A Reformed Baptist view of Baptism, the Covenant, and Children."

Kline, M. G. *By Oath Consigned*. Grand Rapids: Eerdmans, 1968.
Favors infant baptism; relates the rite to covenant ceremonies of ancient Near East.

*MacDonald, A. J., ed. *The Evangelical Doctrine of Holy Communion*. Cambridge: W. Heffer and Son, 1936.
A valuable historical study by evangelical scholars in the Church of England. Contains bibliographies.

Marcel, Pierre. *The Biblical Doctrine of Infant Baptism*. London: James Clarke, 1953.
An extensive argument for infant baptism by a French Calvinist.

Stone, Darwell. *A History of the Doctrine of the Holy Eucharist*. London: Longmans and Green, 1909.
A comprehensive survey of the history of the doctrine.

Eschatology

Allis, Oswald T. *Prophecy and the Church*. Philadelphia: Presbyterian and Reformed, 1945.

Criticism of dispensationalism; amillennial.

Bass, Clarence. *Backgrounds to Dispensationalism*. Grand Rapids: Eerdmans, 1960.
A fine survey and critical analysis of dispensationalism.

Berkhof, Louis. *Systematic Theology*. Grand Rapids: Eerdmans, 1941.
See the section on eschatology for a presentation of the amillennial view.

*Berkouwer, G. C. *The Return of Christ*. Grand Rapids: Eerdmans, 1972.
Good discussion of a broad range of eschatological issues; amillennial.

Boettner, Loraine. *The Millennium*. Philadelphia: Presbyterian and Reformed, 1957.
Postmillennial.

Brown, David. *Christ's Second Coming*. 6th ed. Edinburgh: Clark, 1867.
Postmillennial. Old but still valuable.

Campbell, Roderick. *Israel and the New Covenant*. Philadelphia: Presbyterian and Reformed, 1954.
A postmillennial view of Israel and Old Testament prophecy.

Chafer, Lewis Sperry. *Systematic Theology*. Dallas: Dallas Seminary Press, 1947-1948.
Volume 4 deals with eschatology; dispensational.

*Clouse, Robert G., ed., *The Meaning of the Millennium*. Downers Grove, IL: Inter-Varsity, 1977.
A very helpful symposium of four millennial views.

Cohn, Norman. *The Pursuit of the Millennium*. New York: Oxford University Press, 1970.
A study of millenarian thought during the Middle Ages; suggests analogies with modern revolutionary social movements.

Erickson, Millard J. *Contemporary Options in Eschatology*. Grand Rapids: Baker, 1977.
A helpful survey of the major views. Premillennial, posttribulational.

Froom, Leroy. *The Prophetic Faith of Our Fathers.* Washington, DC: Review and Herald, 1946-1954.

A four-volume history of prophetic interpretation written by a Seventh-Day Adventist; contains much otherwise obscure information.

Frost, Henry W. *The Second Coming of Christ.* Grand Rapids: Eerdmans, 1934.

A survey of biblical data from a premillennial perspective.

Hodge, Charles. *Systematic Theology.* New York: Scribner, 1871.

See volume 3 for a postmillennial outlook.

*Kik, J. Marcellus. *An Eschatology of Victory.* Nutley, NJ: Presbyterian and Reformed, 1974.

Especially valuable for exegesis of Matthew 24; postmillennial.

Klausner, Joseph. *The Messianic Idea in Israel.* New York: Macmillan, 1958.

A definitive study by a noted Jewish scholar. Note appendix, "The Jewish and Christian Messiah."

Ladd, George E. *The Blessed Hope.* Grand Rapids: Eerdmans, 1956.

Evangelical criticism of pretribulational-rapture doctrine. See also *Crucial Questions About the Kingdom of God, The Gospel of the Kingdom,* and *The Presence of the Future* by the same author.

Morris, Leon. *Apocalyptic.* Grand Rapids: Eerdmans, 1972.

A brief but helpful study of apocalyptic in the New Testament.

*Murray, Iain. *The Puritan Hope.* London: Banner of Truth, 1971.

An important study of the impact of the postmillenarian hope in Puritanism on the cause of Protestant missions.

Pache, René. *The Return of Jesus Christ.* Chicago: Moody, 1955.

A study of the second coming; dispensational.

Payne, J. Barton. *Encyclopedia of Biblical Prophecy.* New York: Harper and Row, 1973.

A comprehensive reference work written from a premillennial perspective.

Pentecost, J. Dwight. *Prophecy for Today*. Grand Rapids: Zondervan, 1961.
Dispensational. See also *Things to Come* by the same author.

Reese, Alexander. *The Approaching Advent of Christ*. London: Marshall, Morgan, and Scott, 1937.
A scholarly criticism of the views of J. N. Darby from the perspective of classical premillennialism.

Ryrie, Charles C. *Dispensationalism Today*. Chicago: Moody, 1965.
Perhaps the best recent exposition of the dispensational point of view.

Scofield, C. I. *Rightly Dividing the Word of Truth*. New York: Fleming H. Revell, 1907.
Scofield did much to popularize the dispensational view. See also the notes in *The Scofield Reference Bible* (1909) and *The New Scofield Bible* (1967).

Strong, A. H. *Systematic Theology*. Valley Forge, PA: Judson, 1907.
Volume 3 on eschatology argues for a postmillennial view.

Toon, Peter, ed. *Puritans, the Millennium and the Future of Israel*. Cambridge: James Clarke, 1970.
A series of essays on Puritan eschatology from 1600 to 1660.

Vos, Geerhardus. *The Pauline Eschatology*. Grand Rapids: Eerdmans, 1930.
Valuable exegetical discussions; amillennial.

Walvoord, John F. *The Millennial Kingdom*. Findlay, OH: Dunham, 1959.
Dispensational. See also *The Rapture Question* (1957) by the same author.

*Warfield, B. B. *Biblical Doctrines*. New York: Oxford University Press, 1929.
See especially the chapter "The Prophecies of St. Paul" for a postmillennial interpretation of I Corinthians 15:20-28.